The Bollywood Pocketbook of Iconic Dates

Diptakirti Chaudhuri is a marketer by day and a writer by night. He is passionate about and writes on Hindi cinema. He has written six books including three on Bollywood trivia, one on the history of Bollywood and one on legendary screenwriters Salim–Javed. He divides his time between his family in Bangalore and his work in Pune. Outside of real life, he can be found at his blog (diptakirti.com) and on Twitter (@diptakirti).

The Bollywood Pocketbook of Iconic Dates

Diptakirti Chaudhuri

First published in 2022 by Hachette India
(Registered name: Hachette Book Publishing India Pvt. Ltd)
An Hachette UK company
www.hachetteindia.com

1

ISBN 978-93-91028-32-9

Hachette Book Publishing India Pvt. Ltd
4th & 5th Floors, Corporate Centre,
Plot No. 94, Sector 44, Gurugram – 122003, India

Typeset in Arno Pro 11/16
Typeset by InoSoft Systems, Noida

Printed and bound in India by
Manipal Technologies Limited, Manipal

To Muma and Golu

'Tareekh par tareekh, tareekh par tareekh, tareekh par tareekh, tareekh par tareekh milti rahi hai, lekin insaaf nahin mila…'

– From Rajkumar Santoshi's *Damini*
(written by Sutanu Gupta and Dilip Shukla)

Contents

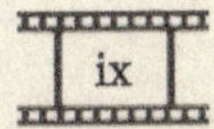

Raja Harishchandra releases

After a premiere to a select audience, *Raja Harishchandra* released as part of a variety programme that also included a dance, a couple of comic acts and a juggling act. The film got great reviews in Bombay (now Mumbai) and moved to smaller towns, where the concept of a 'movie' was completely new. Dhundiraj 'Dadasaheb' Phalke wrote an advertisement: '57,000 photographs of three-quarters of an inch width and two miles length ... all for an anna'. He got his actors to perform street plays to draw in crowds, which took some doing. Neither the making nor the release of the film was smooth.

Phalke went to London for training, and imported a camera and raw film for shooting. His film was fully created in India

– from concept to release. His wife, Saraswatibai,[1] learnt how to develop and process the exposed film, even making the perforations on the side to make them suitable for exhibition. Phalke used Raja Ravi Varma's paintings as inspiration for his frames. And he also managed quite a few innovations in outdoor lighting and special effects (such as making gods appear and disappear). Given the primitive state of technology, these made the first Indian film an object of wonder.

Phalke was a man possessed with the idea of making 'moving pictures' right from the time he watched his first film. It was a film about Jesus Christ, he wanted to bring alive Indian gods and goddesses on the screen. This led to *Raja Harishchandra*. And his involvement touched every aspect of film-making. He coached his cast to do the right facial expressions that were critical for a silent film. He visited Bombay's red-light districts for hiring female actors because no woman from a regular family was allowed to act in films. In a clash of tradition and modernity, male actors playing female parts refused to shave their moustaches because this was only done when one's parent passed away. Phalke got the actors and their fathers together to convince them.

1. She is often called India's first female film technician, for her all-round proficiency in various aspects of film-making.

Beyond film-making, he cast his own son as Harishchandra's son because no one was willing to let their child play a character who died in the movie. During one phase of shooting, his son fell unconscious due to an injury to his head. Since the next shot involved the character being placed on a pyre, and that meant the actor didn't have to move, Phalke went ahead and shot the scene with his unconscious son. In a way, he was like dutiful King Harishchandra, who sacrificed his kingdom and family in pursuit of truth.

When he undertook filming the complicated mythological tale, Phalke claimed the endeavour rather felt like running a factory owned by Harishchandra that employed hundreds of people as cast and crew. And the results of Phalke's single-minded focus to popularize cinema in India are for all to see. India, as a nation, loves cinema – what critics often say – at the cost of every other medium. It is home to some of the world's most thriving film industries. And we have paid our dues to Dadasaheb by naming Indian cinema's highest award after him. Not bad for a factory owner!

Alam Ara releases

Ardeshir Irani could shoot his film only between 1 a.m. and 4 a.m. – local trains in Bombay didn't run between these hours, and some semblance of silence could be achieved. In an era of silent cinema in India, he had watched a Hollywood 'talkie' (*Show Boat* which was only 40 per cent talkie) and decided to make one in India. It was all fine, except that there were no soundproofed studios in India then, nor was the recording equipment required for a soundtrack available. Thus came the night-time shooting schedule. Microphones were hidden in the costumes of the actors, as well as behind props, to record the singing and dialogues. Musicians hid behind the scenery to play the instruments that would form the background music. And thus, India's first talkie was underway.

Ardeshir Irani was a prolific[2] film-maker with his banner, Imperial Films, which eventually birthed legends like Prithviraj Kapoor and Mehboob Khan (who was also considered for the lead role of *Alam Ara*). When he decided to make India's first talkie, he picked up the basics of sound recording from an American working in Bombay's Imperial Theatre and visited London for a couple of weeks to get the hang of things. In the good ol' fashioned jugaad scheme of things, he managed to create a system for recording sound and – in the process – also developed the early version of artificial studio lighting, because even daytime scenes had to be shot indoors, in the dead of the night.

Alam Ara was based on a play by Joseph David Penkar, a popular playwright of Parsi theatre. A kingdom's army chief is imprisoned and his banished wife gives birth to a daughter (who has a locket around her neck, signifying her parentage – oh yes, that familiar thing). The daughter grows up as a gypsy, only to fall in love with the prince of the kingdom. For the title role,

2. And a pioneer too! Irani also produced India's first colour film, *Kisan Kanya*, in 1937, even managing to complete the entire colour processing in India.

Irani chose actress Zubeida over the more popular Sulochana. For the male lead, he chose Master Vithal (known as the Indian Douglas Fairbanks). However, Vithal was contracted to another studio and had to fight a legal battle to get himself released. He hired the services of an England-returned lawyer – Muhammad Ali Jinnah – to fight for his cause. He won the case and eagerly joined the cast of *Alam Ara.*

Alam Ara had seven songs, of which the most popular one was '*De de khuda ke naam pe*' (often called Indian cinema's first song) – performed by actor–singer Wazir Mohammed Khan, playing a fakir in the film. (He went on to play a fakir and sing the same song in two subsequent *Alam Aras,* in 1956 and 1973. Barring some overlaps, the later films were not remakes of the orginal.)

Released in Majestic Theatre with a stampede on day one, *Alam Ara* was advertised as: 'All talking, singing and dancing'. And – expectedly – it became a rage. Speaking stars were a novelty, singing stars even more so. Continuing the tradition of stage performances, Indian cinema embraced song and dance, and did it so completely that nearly a century after *Alam Ara,* our most popular films still can't get away with at least one hit song being performed by the lead players!

Devika Rani debuts, with the longest kiss on Indian screen

The English title of the film was classic Oriental exoticism – *Song of the Serpent*. And the scene was a classic Bollywood cliché. The hero is bitten by a snake and the suggested antidote is that another snake bites him. What happens next is not classic Bollywood fare, even several decades later. When the hero is recovering, his lover falls on him and showers him with kisses for nearly two minutes in one of the most referenced scenes of Hindi cinema. This was the debut of Devika Rani, starring opposite husband Himanshu Rai. The film – titled *Karma* in Hindi – made waves when it premiered in London and the city's swish set was in attendance to welcome the exotic debutante.

We don't give Devika Rani enough credit. She is primarily known as an actress, though her stint as a studio boss[3] is longer (and she has many more credits as a producer than as an actress). Likewise, her contribution to *Karma* went beyond the acting. She wrote the treatment of the film in one evening and that formed the basis of the screenplay. *Karma* was co-produced by Himansurai Indo-International Talkies (serendipitously – or not – abbreviated as HIT!), and the film's international adulation was the reason why Rai and Rani could launch Bombay Talkies the following year.

It all started when they met in London, where she was studying architecture. Rai's flirtatious charm was the ideal foil for Devika Rani's smouldering sensuality. They soon fell in love, and she ended up abandoning her studies for a career in cinema (something frowned upon, in those times). After her debut in *Karma*, she was offered roles in several British productions, but she decided to work in Bollywood, as an equal partner with her husband. She was the face of Bombay Talkies – and maybe even

3. Among her many credits as a studio boss is the discovery of a young Pathan named Yusuf Khan, whom she rechristened 'Dilip Kumar'. All the actors employed with Bombay Talkies had to watch recently released films as part of their study of the medium. Dilip Kumar had once watched *For Whom the Bell Tolls* and submitted his critique to Devika Rani.

early Hindi cinema – because everyone from a commoner to a future prime minister, Jawaharlal Nehru in this case, seemed to be her fan. In an article written in 1939, writer–director K.A. Abbas had attributed Bombay Talkies' meteoric rise to her, 'the only star they have got'.

Devika Rani's biographer, Kishwar Desai, notes in her book *The Longest Kiss* that her relationship with Rai deteriorated quite dramatically, and he even subjected her to grievous verbal and physical abuse. It reached a breaking point when she abandoned a film – *Jeevan Naiya* – midway and ran away to Calcutta (now Kolkata) with her co-star and lover, Najam-ul-Hasan. The plan was to join New Theatres, an up-and-coming studio. With this reckless act, she established who the prime mover of Bombay Talkies was because Rai had to swallow his pride and beg her to return. New Theatres didn't get the boost they could have. Also, Najam-ul-Hasan was replaced in the film with a new actor – Kumudlal Ganguly, or, as we know him better, Ashok Kumar.

We don't give Devika Rani enough credit. For shaping Hindi cinema as we know it today.

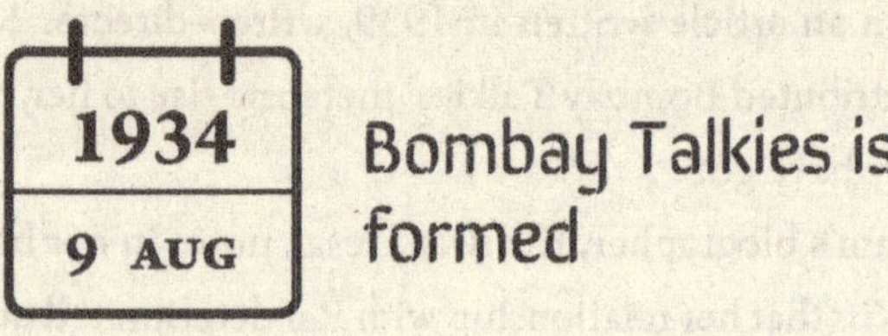

Bombay Talkies is formed

A barrister at Bombay High Court. One of the largest landowners of the city. The head of the Central Bank of India. The founder of Jehangir Art Gallery. One of the city's most prominent stock brokers. The owner of the city's most prominent theatres. These were the kinds of people who were the directors of a new company called The Bombay Talkies Limited with an authorized share capital of ₹25 lakh. An advertisement was released, calling for the public to invest in the company formed 'for the purposes of undertaking the production and exploitation in India and abroad of talking films of various types, for example, entertainment, educational, interest, news and advertising'. Bombay Talkies was formed by the husband–wife duo of Himanshu Rai and Devika Rani. The former was a producer of international repute and the latter a bankable star. Rai went to Europe to study law, but ended up becoming infatuated with the performing arts and stitching together a co-production partnership for a series of films on world religions. Based on his work abroad, he put together a team of international film technicians when Bombay Talkies was formed. Director Franz Osten, cinematographer Josef Wirsching and others worked for the company for several years, creating some of the most iconic films of early Hindi cinema. Bombay Talkies was formed along with other 'talkie studios' of the 1930s like Ranjit Movietone[4] and Sagar Movietone, but neither of them could build and sustain a roster of talent like Bombay Talkies.

Bombay Talkies started by building a studio in Malad with the most modern equipment in place. It replicated the Hollywood model where actors and technicians drew a monthly salary and worked exclusively for the studio. It operated like a factory, and, by 1938, had 400 paid employees working from 9 a.m. to 6 p.m. on films of eventual repute.

4. Like Bombay Talkies, Ranjit Movietone was formed by an entrepreneur–actress, husband–wife pair – Chandulal Shah and Gohar Mamajiwala. They derived their capital from cotton and stock markets, while Gohar was a star actress, an asset for the studio from day one. Ranjit Movietone was a formidable presence in early talkie cinema and outlasted Bombay Talkies in number of years of existence.

Bombay Talkies gave breaks to Ashok Kumar, Dilip Kumar, Madhubala, Leela Chitnis, Mehmood among others. Even Raj Kapoor worked as an assistant here before starting his own studio. After its impactful launch and eventful first years, Himanshu Rai passed away in 1940, but Devika Rani continued to run it along with trusted associates like Sashadhar Mukherjee and Ashok Kumar. Their biggest hit, *Kismet*, happened three years after Rai's death. But ego clashes led to both Mukherjee and Kumar leaving Bombay Talkies to start another studio, Filmistan. They did come back a few years later when Devika Rani handed over the reins to them, but they couldn't revive the studio and it went bankrupt by 1953.

Bombay Talkies was the prime mover in early Hindi cinema, and thanks to their creative and technical excellence, they attracted both money and talent from all over the country. New Theatres (Calcutta) and Prabhat Film Company (Pune), two early players of Indian cinema, started production a few years before Bombay Talkies, but couldn't sustain in the competition against them. Bombay Talkies prevailed, progressed and prospered. When it started, Bombay was just another town – no match to Calcutta, the erstwhile capital of British India. But the studio was instrumental in making the city the nerve centre of Hindi cinema. In short, Bombay Talkies put the 'B' in Bollywood.

Pandit Nehru watches *Achhut Kanya*

The newly formed production company, Bombay Talkies, had made – what it believed – was a film of national importance. The biggest star of the country at that time, Devika Rani, was its lead, along with a newcomer called Ashok Kumar. *Achhut Kanya* highlighted the problem of untouchability in India by showing the love story between a Brahmin boy and an untouchable girl. It was a touchy subject, but given a technically polished treatment (with German technicians handling the direction and photography). The founder of Bombay Talkies, Himanshu Rai, tried to get Mahatma Gandhi to watch his film, which was inspired by the leader's campaign to uplift the people he called Harijan.

However, it was the then Congress president – Jawaharlal Nehru – who came for the premiere at Bombay's Roxy Theatre and watched the film with several Congressmen and women, including Vallabhbhai Patel, Sarojini Naidu and Jamnalal Bajaj. The proceeds of the day's shows were devoted towards the 'upliftment of depressed classes'.

Apart from his duties as the president of Congress to fight against social evils, Nehru was a fan of Devika Rani, which was probably why he agreed to come for the show. It is said that he watched the show sitting between Ashok Kumar and Devika Rani, and even got so excited during a dangerous train sequence that he got up from his seat, forgetting that it was a make-believe scene that was playing out on the screen.

If cinema is indeed expected to be an agent of social change, the Congress president's presence at a socially progressive film would have had a significant impact on the people – about the cause as well as the nascent medium. In fact, using film as a medium for change has always been on Nehru's mind, and he – after becoming the prime minister – used prominent members of the film industry to build awareness about important social issues, raise funds for key projects (for example, the rehabilitation of war widows) and even boost the morale of troops at our borders (which was done by Sunil Dutt's Ajanta

Arts and many other popular stars). Even Lal Bahadur Shastri co-opted Manoj Kumar to spread the message of his slogan '*Jai jawaan, jai kisaan*' through a film (that eventually cemented the actor's cinematic image).

Nehru had written in a letter: 'It is a good film with good photography, and the story is interesting. There is always a danger in films, which have too obvious a moral purpose, to become dull. I find that ... this error is avoided, and there is considerable restraint in dealing with the subject, which is of course of great public importance.' This extract is not from after he watched *Achhut Kanya*, but from nearly two decades later. He had watched Bimal Roy's *Sujata* in June 1959, and was moved enough to compliment the director. But of course, despite cinematic efforts, untouchability was still around.

Prithvi Theatres is founded

Founded by one of the earliest stars of Hindi cinema, Prithvi Theatres is a worthy mascot of the industry's first family – the Kapoors. It is a symbol of the *junoon* that the family displayed in their pursuits, only some of which resulted in becoming classics on celluloid.

Prithviraj Kapoor's first love was the stage, where he was performing to great acclaim right from his school days. He dreamt of having a theatre company even before he joined films. While acting in silent films (from 1929 onwards), he also acted in stage productions (of adaptations of Shakespearean plays and Sanskrit classics) to great acclaim. His presence in major films like *Vidyapati*, *Chingari* and

Sikandar gave him the capital he required to institute Prithvi Theatres.

Prithvi started with a production of *Shakuntala,* but the commercial failure of the play led him to choose contemporary political and social themes for future endeavours. One of his early successes was *Deewaar,* which was about two brothers, one of whom was modelled on Mahatma Gandhi and the other on Muhammad Ali Jinnah. Sardar Vallabhbhai Patel was one of his early inspirations, and his plays touched upon Partition, communalism, the crisis of farmers and so on. The company put up more than 2,600 shows, all of which starred the thespian himself. At its peak, Prithvi Theatres had a cast and crew of more than 100 people, who travelled from town to town, village to village, putting up plays to entertain and inspire the people of the newly formed country. Towards the late 1950s, the charm of a travelling theatre company lost out to a new medium – cinema – and it became impossible to sustain the company. And thus, Prithvi Theatres shut down.

From 1944 to 1960, Prithviraj Kapoor had funded his passion for theatre with his substantial earnings as a top star. His eldest son, Raj Kapoor, made several entertaining films with important social messages through his production company, RK Studios, which was funded by his earnings from acting in several run-of-

the-mill films. His second son, Shammi Kapoor, also contributed towards the expenses of running the theatre company. Shashi Kapoor, the youngest son, went one step further by setting up a film company – Film Valas – with his earnings as a commercial star. Raj Kapoor once jokingly said his youngest brother was a 'taxi', because he was willing to go anywhere for a producer who paid him his fees. Those fees were funding good cinema and – eventually – good theatre. Shashi Kapoor bought the land where Prithviraj Kapoor stayed (called *Prithvi Jhopra*) and built a complex, which he called Prithvi Theatres.

Prithvi Theatres was officially revived in 1978 (on 3 November, Prithviraj's birthday), and has carried on due to his granddaughter Sanjana's efforts. It was no longer a travelling theatre but a performance space and a repertory of arts. Beyond theatre, 'Prithvi' is an iconic cultural spot in today's Mumbai – a place to not only watch but also discuss theatre, and be seen in. It is also where many serious actors and directors hang around, before they get popular enough to get mobbed. The writers of *Gangs of Wasseypur* pitched their script to Anurag Kashyap waiting outside the theatre, when he was presenting a play starring his then wife, Kalki Koechlin. History has been made here in more ways than one.

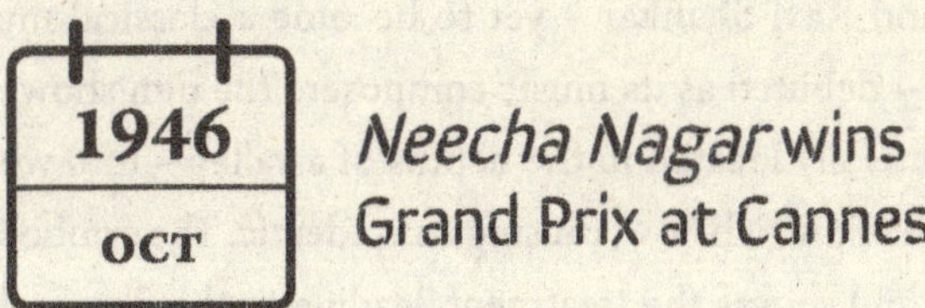

1946 OCT

Neecha Nagar wins Grand Prix at Cannes

Cinematographer Subrata Mitra has an impressive body of work, including all of Satyajit Ray's early films. He once came across cans of film reels in a junk shop that were ready to be burned for the silver nitrate present in celluloid reels. He bought the cans, and discovered it was a print of *Neecha Nagar* – almost forgotten despite being the first Indian film to have won an award at Cannes Film Festival.

Indian People's Theatre Association (IPTA) had delivered many message-driven plays on stage, and they were also looking to expand to the screen. *Neecha Nagar* was one of their first efforts. Writer Khwaja Ahmad Abbas (who would soon find fame as the writer of Raj Kapoor's classics) wrote the script based on a story by Hayatullah Ansari, which in turn was inspired by Maxim Gorky's *Lower Depths.* It was Chetan Anand's first directorial venture and Ravi Shankar – yet to become a classical music superstar – debuted as its music composer. The film showed a village – literally located in the depths of a valley – into which the sewage of the rich flow, causing an epidemic. The symbolism was stark and so was the treatment, leading to the film finding no takers in India. It was entered into the Cannes Film Festival with an unprecedented result.

India has a patchy record at Cannes. In recent times, its presence has largely been restricted to top actresses making appearances on behalf of the global brands they endorse or for Bollywood extravaganzas that aren't part of the prestigious competition. Neeraj Ghaywan's *Masaan* received an extended standing ovation in 2015, but very few Indian films have made the cut at the world's premier film festival. *Neecha Nagar* was one of 11 films to be awarded the festival's top prize in 1946. The winners' list included films like Roberto Rossellini's *Rome, Open City* and David Lean's *Brief Encounter* – long acknowledged as classics of world cinema.

Despite its international recognition, *Neecha Nagar* didn't even find a proper release in India and was reviewed as 'a dismal flop' by *The Times of India*. The reviewer went on to say, 'All I said [to] myself was that if *Neecha Nagar* got a Grand Prix, I shudder to think what the other films were like'!

So how good was *Neecha Nagar* really? When Chetan Anand was struggling to find distributors to release his film, he received a letter in which the writer praised the film and indicated that he was inspired to make his own movie in the same realistic mould. The writer was Satyajit Ray, who made his own mark at Cannes with *Pather Panchali* – about a decade after *Neecha Nagar*.

A present-day winner. The director and cast of *Masaan* at Cannes, where the film won the FIPRESCI prize in the Un Certain Regard section and Promising Future prize (Prix Avenir Prometteur) in 2015.

Image courtesy of Neeraj Ghaywan

Raj Kapoor meets Nargis

Raj Kapoor visited the newly opened Famous Studios in Mahalaxmi, where he wanted to shoot his first film, *Aag*. From there, he went over to veteran producer Jaddanbai's flat in Chateau Marine building on Marine Drive. He was casting for *Aag* and needed a bankable star to play the third heroine in the film. He knew Jaddanbai's daughter was already a star. Raj came over unannounced, and Nargis was busy in the kitchen. She opened the door with her hands covered in *besan* paste. Nargis carelessly pushed back her hair with her hands, and smeared a bit of *besan* on her hair. The vividness of this scene was fresh in Raj's mind for ages because he immortalized it on screen nearly 30 years later. In *Bobby*, Dimple Kapadia opens the door in the same way when Rishi Kapoor appears at her doorstep for the first time.

From that unforgettable first meeting, Raj Kapoor went to his writer Inder Raj Anand's house on Warden Road and said, 'I must have this girl in my film. You must write her into the screenplay.' From that moment on, Nargis and RK were inextricably intertwined. At the beginning of the partnership, Nargis was already a star while Raj was still Prithviraj Kapoor's son trying to make films with a unique mix of desperate penny-pinching, audacious borrowing and unbounded optimism. But their on-screen chemistry made them a pair like no other. By their second film, *Barsaat*, Nargis was part of the RK Films' logo. And by the time they had done *Andaz, Awara, Shree 420* and *Chori*, they were part of industry folklore. Raj Kapoor famously said that his wife was the mother of his children, while Nargis the mother of his films.

Raj Kapoor and Nargis were also in love. During the shooting of *Aag*, Nargis had confided to her friend that 'Pinkie has started getting fresh with me'. But she was soon swept away by his charm, and according to rumours, Raj Kapoor had even tied a symbolic mangalsutra around her neck on New Year's Eve of 1950. Nargis tried to formalize the relationship by requesting the then home minister of Bombay, Morarji Desai, to assist

her in legally marrying Raj Kapoor, but nothing came out of it.

Such was her impact that Raj Kapoor's heroines came to be known as the 'Women in White' for being the pristine beacon of morality (apart from the colour of the sarees they all wore). Thanks to her presence, Raj Kapoor's early films not only made big money at the box office, they were also socially relevant and important films. After she left him, his camera treated his heroines more voyeuristically and his affairs with them continued unabated. While she found love and a durable marriage with Sunil Dutt.

Their end was as dramatic as their beginning. Raj once found Nargis reading a letter. When he asked her about it, she tore up the letter and threw it away. An insecure Raj returned to the room later, retrieved the letter from the bin and pieced it together. It was a proposal for a film from a producer, which she was keeping away from him. Like the first meeting, their break-up was also immortalized in a RK film – *Sangam*.

A painting by René Francois Prinet could well have been the inspiration behind the iconic RK Films logo, which had a woman (Nargis) wilting dramatically in the arms of a man (Raj Kapoor) holding a violin.

'The Kreutzer Sonata' by René-Xavier Prinet. Sotheby's, New York, 19th Century European Paintings, Drawings & Sculpture, 12 October 1994 Lot 146. Wikimedia Commons.

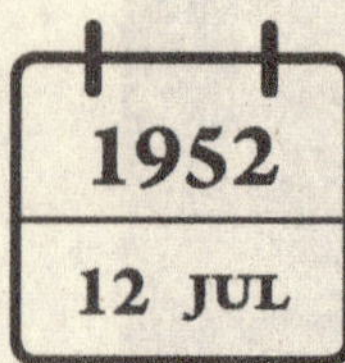

Cinematograph Act is passed, Censor Board is formed

Red-light districts of Mumbai. Nuclear testing sites. Riot victims. Death of a dacoit. Intercourse (the word, not the act). Lady oriented story (sic). Savita Bhabhi. Lesbian (again, the word). Homosexuality (yes, the word). Overflowing toilet. Images of Goddess Kali and Lakshmi.[5]

All of the above seemingly disjointed phrases have one thing in common – India's much-feared, much-reviled censors have

---

5. These transgressions are from the following films: K.A. Abbas' *Char Shaher Ek Kahani*. Anand Patwardhan's *Jang Aur Aman*. Ramesh Pimple's *Aakrosh*. Ramesh Sippy's *Sholay*. Imtiaz Ali's *Jab Harry Met Sejal*. Alankrita Shrivastava's *Lipstick Under My Burkha*. Nitya Mehra's *Baar Baar Dekho*. Sharat Katariya's *Dum Laga Ke Haisha*. Hansal Mehta's *Aligarh*. Rajkumar Hirani's *Sanju*. Pan Nalin's *Angry Indian Goddesses*.

at least objected to them, if not managed to remove them from the films altogether. The journey started in newly independent India. After many years of dodging British censors to pass nationalistic messages, one would have expected the country to do differently, but well...

The Cinematograph Act of 1952 – called the Bible of film censorship in India – wasn't the first set of laws to regulate the film industry. The first censorship laws were introduced in 1918 and regional censor boards were formed to keep in check the nationalistic outputs of Indian film-makers. Post-Independence, the new Act integrated the regional censor boards under a central board – the Central Board of Film Certification (CBFC) – with a chairman and advisory committees (as it stands today). And proceeded to frame censorship rules that treated the entire population of India as children.

Lilavati Munshi, a Rajya Sabha MP, formed a Society for Prevention of Unhealthy Trends in Motion Pictures in the early 1950s, and regularly wrote petitions to remove obscenity from cinema. One of these was addressed to PM Nehru where 13,000 Delhi housewives signed the petition. Another was to Mamie Eisenhower (then First Lady of USA) to ask her to 'stop the production of such Hollywood films' which were ruining the 'moral fibre of younger generations'. The continued debauched output of Hollywood indicates Mamie Eisenhower didn't do much, while it is said that kissing and nudity – often visible in the films in the 1920s and 1930s – almost dwindled to zero on Indian screens, thanks to Mrs Munshi's efforts.

Partly because of the puritanism of our early leaders (who thought nothing of banning film music from our national broadcaster), partly due to our societal conservatism and partly due to our mistrust of the type of people who worked in cinema, film censorship was widely supported and hence assiduously exercised by the CBFC. For the last 70 years, censorship has been a hot topic – often getting national prominence over a film or a display of double standards. The legendary Helen famously said, 'I've spent my whole career dancing between a pair of scissors', and *Life* magazine was intrigued enough to do a story on 'India's Kissing Crisis' in the late 1960s when there was a national furore on whether liplocks should be allowed in films or not.

CBFC has often been accused of political posturing, favouritism and even corruption for its decisions. And those decisions, collectively, could well be the reason why India continues to be such a repressed society. 'Why do you think we have so much vulgarity, songs, dances, pelvic thrusts, bathtub fantasies and dream sequences? Because you won't allow a simple kiss,' said an exasperated stakeholder on India's paranoid, complicated and immature censorship policies. The person was Vijay Anand, chairman of CBFC between 2001 and 2002.

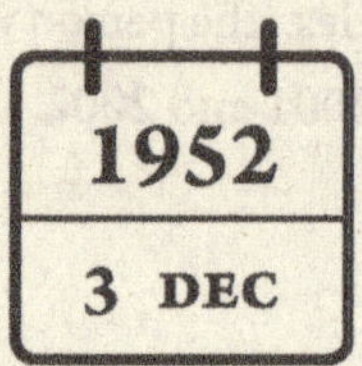

Binaca Geetmala is born

'*Bhaiyo aur beheno,*' said Ameen Sayani and walked into the collective consciousness of our nation. And kept walking till his signature introduction became part of the lives of several generations. It all started with *Binaca Geetmala*. It didn't start in India, though – strictly speaking!

India's third information and broadcasting minister, B.V. Keskar, banned several things from All India Radio, including cricket commentary (because it was a British game) and Hindi film songs (because he considered them too Westernized and vulgar). This was exploited by Radio Ceylon – Asia's oldest radio station, in Sri Lanka – whose Hindi service overflowed with film songs, the crowning glory of which was *Binaca Geetmala*.

The first countdown show of Hindi film songs, it started after *Binaca Hit Parade* – a countdown of English pop music – was launched on Radio Ceylon, and the station was flooded with requests for a Hindi version. Initially, the show played only seven popular songs of the day without ranking them, but it soon became a countdown. The ranking process involved a complex mix of record sales and feedback from *shrota sangathans* – because sales figures weren't reliable when stores ran out of popular records. The *shrota sangathans* were clubs of listeners, spread all over the country. They wrote feedback about the popular songs of the day, and were instrumental in building both the rankings and the programme's following.

The loss of revenue and listeners forced All India Radio to launch the Vividh Bharati service (on 2 October 1957) and *Binaca Geetmala* moved there, only to became even more popular, with over 20 crore listeners at its peak. *Binaca Geetmala* remained the benchmark of popularity among Hindi songs, sparking cheers, debates and heartbreaks with the ranking of their songs. Conspiracy theories abounded among the public, and even music directors accused each other of rigging the rankings. It was such a big issue that an ombudsman from the industry was appointed to 'approve' the ratings and check for any bias! (Producer G.P. Sippy was the first ombudsman.)

From '*Yeh zindagi usi ki hai*' (*Anarkali*) to '*Choli ke peechhe*' (*Khal Nayak*), from Lata Mangeshkar to Alka Yagnik (and Ila Arun), from Talat Mehmood (singing '*Jaaye toh jaaye kahan*' in *Taxi Driver*) to Kumar Sanu (singing '*Maine pyar tumhi se*' in *Phool Aur Kaante*), it has also been an extremely durable barometer of our love for film songs. In fact, what better way to demonstrate its durability and popularity than the fact that the sponsor changed names twice, but didn't give away the naming rights till the end! Toothpaste brand Binaca became Cibaca and was then acquired by a different company to become Colgate Cibaca, but Geetmala played on!

The popularity continued unabated till 1994, when video killed the radio star. With the launch of Doordarshan (DD) Metro, *Binaca Geetmala* ended its run after getting upstaged by television's first ever countdown show...*Superhit Muqabla*!

Russia hosts the Indian Film Festival

Stalin died in 1953. During his regime – specifically under Minister of Culture Andrei Zhdanov – all art forms were supervised and asked to adhere to socialist realism. With Stalin's death, a stronger cultural relationship with India started, and with it, Russia developed a taste for '*Indiiskie melodramy*' (Indian melodramas). Realistic Indian dramas were being imported by Soviet Russia in the early years of Indian independence. The Soviet film import/export department had set up an office in Bombay, and films like *Dharti Ke Lal* and *Chinnamul* were the first Indian films to be purchased for Soviet theatres. However, they were focused on social messages and didn't catch the imagination of the

Russian audience. That changed with the Indian Film Festival of 1954.

An estimated 1 million viewers watched films at the festival that was organized in Moscow and four other cities. The films shown included Raj Kapoor's *Awara*, Bimal Roy's *Do Bigha Zamin*, Chetan Anand's *Aandhiyan* and K.A. Abbas's *Rahi*. The festival was attended by major stars like Raj Kapoor, Nargis, Dev Anand, Nirupa Roy and Durga Khote. Audiences thronged the venues, and lapped up the films along with the dance shows and art exhibitions that happened before the screenings. Raj Kapoor and Nargis became an instant hit, with Raj's character of the lovable tramp finding fans all over Soviet Russia. Not only the common people, even political leaders and celebrities were fans of Indian film stars. Writer–director K.A. Abbas interviewed astronaut Yuri Gagarin and ended up writing a book on him.

This festival was the trigger behind the adulation Hindi films received in Soviet Russia, which remained one Indian cinema's most lucrative markets for decades. *Awara* was not only the highest-grossing foreign language film of the year (with nearly 64 million viewers), it also became an enduring phenomenon. Thanks to *Awara*, Raj Kapoor inserted a nod towards his Russian fan base in his next film (*Shree 420*): '*Sar pe laal topi Russi*' and the rights were sold at an unusually high price. By this time, Raj

Kapoor was a pan-Russia star, and was in direct contact with the minister of culture. Going forward, the escapist musical melodramas of Bollywood ruled the roost from the 1960s to the 1970s. Films like *Love in Simla, Ganga Jumna, Aradhana, Bobby* and *Seeta Aur Geeta* were major grossers in Soviet Russia. In the 1980s, *Disco Dancer* released, and its phenomenal popularity in Russia ensured it became the first Hindi film to gross ₹100–crore worldwide, a box-office benchmark that only became common 20 years later.

From 1954 till the Soviet Russia broke into independent countries, the dazzling charm of Hindi films wowed generations of audiences, who went from the greys of their gritty films to the multi-coloured hues of Bollywood. As a fan once said, 'I remember vividly the colour of Rekha's sari … apple green. In our grey lives, we literally happened into a fantasy world... I had never seen anything like this.' Indeed, Bollywood does that to you.

Dilip Kumar faces Madhubala in a court of law

'In the name of god, I ask you whether you are in love with Madhubala?' the prosecuting attorney asked.

'I too loved her; it was a mutual feeling,' the biggest star in the country replied in a packed courtroom.

This dramatic exchange was not a film, but a real case, filed by B.R. Films against Madhubala, whom they accused of breach of contract. But the story went back further than that.

Madhubala and Dilip Kumar had met when she was just a child, but they fell in love on the sets of *Tarana*. Their magnum opus – *Mughal-e-Azam* – started filming around the same time (1951), and the film's director, K. Asif, supported their relationship. Dilip Kumar spoke of her with candid affection in his autobiography: 'She ... was very sprightly and vivacious and, as such, she could draw me out of my shyness and reticence effortlessly.' However, when the relationship reached Madhubala's father for his approval, he put down commercial conditions that were unacceptable to Dilip Kumar. It is said that he wanted them to act exclusively for a production house floated by him. Dilip Kumar refused to proceed in a relationship that, seemingly, was becoming a business venture.

By this time, Dilip Kumar and Madhubala had started shooting for B.R. Films' *Naya Daur*, but Madhubala's father refused to allow his daughter to go for outdoor shoots with her now-estranged lover. After the production house pleaded with him and failed, they filed a case against them for not fulfilling their contractual obligations. Madhubala's father filed a counter-claim that the case was instigated by Dilip Kumar, who was called a 'jilted lover' in court by the defence lawyer. He was also accused of misbehaving with Madhubala in the past, sometimes under the influence of alcohol. It was also claimed that the film could easily be shot indoors, and that the outdoor shoot wasn't necessary.

It was a sensational case and Dilip Kumar – the greatest actor of his generation – had the opportunity to present his side of the story on a stage far bigger than what any film would give him. He took to the witness stand and supported B.R. Films' assertion about unprofessionalism on part of the actress and her father. The case carried on for a year, and the film had released by then. The judge on the case, Justice R.S. Parikh came to see *Naya Daur* and was convinced that it wasn't a film that could be shot entirely indoors. He gave a verdict in favour of the producers, who then chose to end the matter, and not ask for Madhubala and her father's prosecution.

The case underscored an important point about the professionalism (or lack of it) in the film industry, and pitted two of the country's biggest stars against each other. But what it destroyed completely was the Dilip Kumar–Madhubala love story. They separated, even while shooting what would become their biggest success – *Mughal-e-Azam*. When the famous scene in which Salim caresses Anarkali with a feather was being filmed, the two weren't even on speaking terms. Sigh.

Lata Mangeshkar sings *'Ae Mere Watan Ke Logon'*

'*Beti, aaj tumne mujhe rula diya,*' the sitting prime minister told the singer after her performance. And for good reason too! India had lost its war with China in 1962, and much of the blame was laid at Prime Minister Nehru's door – for his diplomacy being unable to anticipate the Chinese response to border disputes and for his defence strategy being unable to put up a proper frontline response.

Anyway, the war had ended with defeat for India, and massive fundraising initiatives were being organized to support the casualties of the war.

Kavi Pradeep (born Ramchandra Dwivedi) was not among the leading lyricists of the industry then, but his credentials for patriotic song writing was beyond doubt. '*Chal chal re naujawan*' (*Bandhan*), '*Ao bachche tumhe dikhayein jhanki Hindustan ki*' and '*De di humein azaadi bina khadag bina dhal*' (both from *Jagriti*) were superhit patriotic songs. At the height of the freedom struggle, he had also written '*Door hato ae duniyawalon, Hindustan humara hai*' (*Kismet*), which escaped the British censor's scissors by claiming that India was asking the rest of the world (that is, the Axis powers) to stay away from the country.

This time, Pradeep was approached by film-maker Mehboob Khan to pen the lyrics for a major fundraising event in Delhi. The lyrics of the song had come to Pradeep while he was strolling on the beach and he borrowed a passer-by's pen to write down the first stanza on the foil of a cigarette pack. Mehboob got C. Ramachandra to compose the tune and approached Lata Mangeshkar to sing. She almost dropped out from the song because her busy schedule didn't leave her with enough time to rehearse for it. She was convinced to perform because Pradeep insisted on having her. The lyricist didn't even want Asha Bhosle to perform it as a duet with her sister. Lata tried to make up for the lack of rehearsals by repeatedly listening to a recording of Ramachandra's rendition of the song, even when she was on the flight to Delhi.

The show was organized as a part of India's Republic Day celebrations, and was attended by President S. Radhakrishnan and Prime Minister Nehru, along with a massive crowd. After the song was performed, there wasn't a single dry eye in the audience. And the song went on to become one of our most iconic patriotic anthems.

Lata Mangeshkar, of course, went on to become India's best-known music personality. Kavi Pradeep was accorded the title of 'Rashtrakavi', one among a handful of poets to be so honoured. Strangely, he was not invited to the function in Delhi, and only got a chance to perform his own work in front of Nehru when the prime minister visited Bombay a couple of months later. Nevertheless, he remains one of the those few writers whose work has reached an entire nation and helped people come to terms with their grief.

Guru Dutt passes away

'Send the child or you will see my dead body,' Guru Dutt said to his estranged wife, Geeta, on the phone. He wanted his daughter, Nina, to be sent across to his Ark Royal apartment on Pedder Road, but Geeta wasn't inclined to do so. Writer-director Abrar Alvi was working on the last scene of the next Guru Dutt production, *Baharen Phir Bhi Aayengi*, struggling to write a tragic scene in which the heroine dies. Because of this scene what Guru Dutt said to his wife stuck, but Alvi didn't pay it much attention. After all, people say these things when they are angry and tipsy.

Guru Dutt was drinking since 5.30 in the evening, chatting with a friend who had come over. He had called Raj Kapoor too, asking him to come over the next day as he wanted to show him his last directorial venture, *Kaagaz Ke Phool.* Abrar Alvi finished the scene and had dinner, while Guru Dutt continued to drink, and left around midnight. At around 3 a.m., Guru Dutt took one more bottle of whiskey into his bedroom and locked the door from inside. He was discovered dead the following morning when Geeta Dutt called repeatedly and eventually asked his house help, Ratan, to break open the door.

Guru Dutt was remarkably sensitive. His work, his loves and his passions consumed him. Over the last few years of his life, he suffered several professional and personal setbacks. His magnum opus *Kaagaz Ke Phool* performed disastrously at the box office, causing him so much pain that he refused to lend his name as director to his subsequent films. Severe discord had set in his marriage with Geeta Dutt. It was the souring of a passionate love story – as evidenced by his many letters to her – between two talented but emotionally fragile individuals. The marriage was affected by Guru Dutt's love for his co-star, Waheeda Rehman, who had ended their relationship about a year ago. That his latest production, *Baharen Phir Bhi Aayengi,* wasn't shaping up well was probably the last straw.

All this led to the overdose of Sonaril tablets, which he had crushed and dissolved in water. *Filmfare*'s cover story summed up the tragedy in three words: *Khuda, Maut aur Ghulam*.

Guru Dutt was only 39 years old when he passed away. Journalist Bunny Reuben wrote, 'Not just Guru Dutt died. That day, a part of the soul of every sensitive man died. A part of the future of Indian cinema died.' Guru Dutt left behind an impressive body of work, and probably an even more impactful filmography remained undone. His films like *Baazi*, *Jaal*, *Aar-Paar*, *Mr & Mrs '55*, *Pyaasa*, *Chaudhvin Ka Chand* and *Sahib Bibi Aur Ghulam* were not only box-office successes, but milestones of Hindi cinema. They inspired talented youngsters from all over the country to embark on a journey into the industry. Less than a week before his death, one such youngster had arrived in Bombay hoping to become a director like Guru Dutt. He was devastated when he heard about his idol's death on a radio playing in a roadside shop. His heart broke, but not his will. His name was Javed Akhtar.

Sharmila Tagore appears on the *Filmfare* cover, in a bikini

When Sharmila Tagore walked into the studio of photographer Dhiraj Chawda for a photo shoot, she was carrying just a handbag. When the photographer asked where her costumes for the shoot were, she coolly pulled out a floral-print bikini from her bag. 'Are you sure about this?' he asked, and was much more uncomfortable about the shoot than Tagore herself. For some of the shots, he even asked her to cover up a bit. And thus, India's first bikini cover was born.

Sharmila Tagore had made her debut as a teenager in Satyajit Ray's acclaimed Bengali films *Apur Sansar* and *Devi,* where she played demure housewives in sarees. Her Hindi debut was in Shakti Samanta's *Kashmir Ki Kali,* where she was in *pherans* and salwar–kameezes all through. But Bollywood was becoming glamourous and going international in the mid-1960s, with Hollywood influencing it in a big way. International locations were becoming a trend after *Sangam* became the first Indian film to be shot in Europe. In Yash Chopra's *Waqt*, fashionable clothes were a big part of the film's draw and Sadhana (along with Sunil Dutt) appeared in a swimsuit in an extended pool scene.

The occasion for the *Filmfare* cover was Shakti Samanta's upcoming film *An Evening in Paris*, where – as per the August 1966 magazine issue – 'Sharmila Tagore has to wear a bikini. The scenes are to be shot in the French Riviera. Before she flew out for the filming, Sharmila gave us a preview of the costume – some beachwear and a lot of Sharmila'. While heroines were seen in swimsuits before,[6] she became the first Indian heroine to be seen in a bikini.

As happens in India even now, the uproar about the cover was immediate and widespread. People thought a bikini-clad *Bharatiya naari* was scandalous, and it is said that some political parties even raised the issue in Parliament! The outrage rattled

6. Nargis and Nutan were stars when they appeared in swimsuits in *Awara* and *Dilli Ka Thug* respectively. The first Indian actress to sport a swimsuit – way back in 1938 – was Meenakshi in *Brahmachari*. Meenakshi's two granddaughters also joined films later – Shilpa and Namrata Shirodkar.

Sharmila Tagore a fair bit, but she calmed down when her then boyfriend, Mansoor Ali Khan Pataudi (who was playing county cricket in Sussex), telegrammed her: 'Relax! You could only be looking very nice!'

Thanks to the outrage, the scene in *An Evening in Paris* was shot with Tagore wearing a single-piece swimming costume instead of the more revealing bikini. She was seen water surfing in the blue costume in Beirut in the song '*Aasmaan se aaya farishta*'. Despite the outrage, the cover and the film became hugely popular, and – of course – Tagore went on to become a top heroine, known for both conservative and sensuous roles. The trend slowly started picking up and, by the early 1970s, we had Dimple Kapadia in *Bobby* and Zeenat Aman in *Heera Panna* scorching the screen in two-pieces.

Life came a full circle when Sharmila Tagore's (then to-be) daughter-in-law, Kareena Kapoor, and daughter, Soha Ali Khan, appeared in bikinis, in *Tashan* and *Mr Joe B. Carvalho* respectively. Given the predictability of Indian media, both were asked how they felt. Funnily, even Tagore was asked the same question 40 years ago. And how did she feel? 'Oh, rather like a pioneer,' she had replied. Indeed!

Manoj Kumar plays Bharat in *Upkar*

Manoj Kumar had ghost directed *Shaheed*, his first patriotic film, in which he played freedom fighter Bhagat Singh. He travelled to Delhi for a special screening with the then prime minister, Lal Bahadur Shastri. The prime minister, after a successful but difficult war against Pakistan, had coined the inspirational slogan '*Jai jawaan, jai kisaan*'. He loved *Shaheed* enough to call Kumar at 2 a.m., invite him for tea the next day and request the actor if he could make a film on the slogan. Manoj Kumar was so enthused by the request that he wrote the first draft of the script on his train journey back to Bombay. And his name in the film was Bharat. (If the connection was not clear enough, the film was advertised as 'The Story of a Man and a Land – Both Named Bharat'.)

Upkar was described by Manoj Kumar himself as a '16,000-feet long celluloid flag of India'. He plays a farmer who goes to the front (in the 1965 war against Pakistan) – thus becoming both a jawaan and kisaan – and comes back to reform his foreign-returned brother (Prem Chopra) from falling into a life of crime with black marketers. If that wasn't patriotism personified, Asha Parekh plays a doctor promoting family planning in the village. And, in his first positive role, Pran plays Malang Chacha – a handicapped war veteran – who brought in the uncomfortable angle about India's poor treatment of its war heroes (though not overtly).

The reviews were somewhat guarded. While praising the effort to eulogize farmers and soldiers, *The Times of India* said '*Upkar* flourishes slogans and sermons with almost the unabashed directness of commissioned job for the Films Division'. This was not inaccurate because the messaging was triggered by the prime minister, and several state governments exempted the film from entertainment tax for 'its national and social significance'. What was not guarded though was the audience reaction. *Upkar* was one of the highest-grossing films of the year, and picked up six Filmfare awards, including Best Story, Dialogues, Direction

and Film. At the National Awards, it bagged the prize for the second-best feature film.

But none of these awards quite capture the impact *Upkar* had. Beyond its box-office run, the film had probably the most famous patriotic film song. Written by Gulshan Bawra, composed by Kalyanji–Anandji and lustily sung by Mahendra Kapoor, '*Mere desh ki dharti sona ugle, ugle heere moti*' played in school functions, on national holidays and every conceivable patriotic occasion. Decades after *Upkar*, the song still remains a staple on All India Radio and Doordarshan – thus living on for generations. It also ignited Manoj Kumar's patriotic fervour. Right after its release, film industry folks and the media started referring to him as 'Mr Bharat'. The name stuck, and in all the films he directed and produced thereafter, Manoj Kumar's name was Bharat and patriotism became his calling card. Be it seriously or as a spoof, Manoj Kumar was nothing but Bharat.

A new actor is signed for *Saat Hindustani*

One young man left a film for a stint in Calcutta. And he was replaced by another young man coming in from Calcutta. Tinnu Anand had got an opportunity to assist legendary director Satyajit Ray, for which he decided to give up an acting role he was selected for in Khwaja Ahmad Abbas' *Saat Hindustani*. His role went to a corporate executive, who had given up a lucrative job in Calcutta to try his luck in Bollywood. This young man was offered ₹5,000 for the entire film – requiring several months of work – while he was getting a salary of Rs 1,600 per month at his cushy job. Crazy is not an adjective we normally associate with Amitabh Bachchan – but maybe we should here.

Amitabh Bachchan worked for two firms in Calcutta, which ran paper mills, coal mines, as well as freight broking. Staying in a chummery on the posh Little Russell Street and driving a second-hand Fiat, he lived the good life in independent India's most happening city. He was also part of a theatre group, The Amateurs, thanks to an acting bug he nurtured from his school and college days. He acted in an adaptation of *Who's Afraid of Virginia Woolf?*, though a reviewer called his movements 'awkward'. During this time, he also did a two-minute voice-over for director Mrinal Sen's *Bhuvan Shome* – receiving ₹300 for his efforts. He posed – rather morosely – at Calcutta's Victoria Memorial for his brother, Ajitabh, to click some photographs, and sent them for various talent hunt competitions, receiving no response. One such photo reached Abbas and he was called for a meeting. When asked why he was rejected by other directors, the lanky young man said candidly, 'They all said I was too tall for their heroines.'

Saat Hindustani was low-profile debut for Amitabh, and did nothing for his career. At best, it was his symbolic beginning in the film world and kicked off four years of backbreaking struggle, debilitating failures and innumerable rejections. His fabled baritone didn't find any takers, his tall frame was considered awkward, and his brooding intensity too serious for the happy romances of the time. His is the most famous struggle of Bollywood, the proverbial outsider who fought his way to the top. He was the son of noted poet Harivansh Rai Bachchan, and a family friend of the then prime minister, Indira Gandhi, and yet, never used any of those connections in the film world. The struggle has the added dimension of Amitabh leaving behind a high-paying job, only to end up sleeping on a Marine Drive bench on a few occasions. He recounted later that in his corporate job, he was managing the profile of people who would be rudely rejecting him for various roles.

Many heroes and heroines have waited for the right film. In Amitabh's case though, he had to wait for the mood of the nation to change. The country's dominant state of mind changed from mushy romance to searing anger, before a police officer could look a gangster in the eye and drive an entire generation crazy. Crazy is not an adjective we associate with Amitabh Bachchan – but we should.

Stardust releases

'Is Rajesh Khanna married?' The cover story was run along with an unflattering photo of the actor. This was at a time when 'The Phenomenon' could do no wrong. The story was sourced from Anju Mahendru (who was dating Khanna at that time) and her mother, both of whom wanted to put pressure on him to marry her. This cover story was enough for the first issue of *Stardust* to sell out its first print run of 25,000 copies in less than a week. And with that, a new brand of bitchy, gossipy, chatty, racy film journalism was born.

Founder Nari Hira moved Shobhaa Rajadhyaksha (later De) – a copywriter of his ad agency – as the first editor of *Stardust*, and they made up the rules of journalism as they went along.

Nari Hira called the other film magazines of the times 'PR magazines', because they featured 'Waheeda Rehman, Nanda and Sadhana making sand castles on Juhu beach'.[7] *Stardust*, on the other hand, spared no one, scooped industry scandals and remained a catty outsider, uninterested in the glamour that the industry peddled. Shobhaa De didn't attend shoots, parties or muhurats. Her journalists were also not from the regular filmi beat, but people who weren't awed by the stars they covered.

The result was unabashedly snarky and wicked copy, written in Hinglish, and with a tongue firmly in cheek. Their opening column of gossip snippets – Neeta's Natter – was inspired by Hollywood gossip queen Hedda Hopper's style, but the lingo was unmistakably Indian. *Stardust* coined many of the nicknames we use even now – Garam Dharam, Shotgun Sinha (for Shatrughan Sinha's verbosity), Idli Malini (presumably for Hema's South Indian origins and fair complexion), La Tagore (for Sharmila's la-de-dah style) and *snigger* Asli Ghee (for Yogita Bali's chubby looks)! The journalists faced lawsuits on a regular basis and played out the adjournment game in courts

7. Since we are on Juhu beach, we can mention that when *Cine Blitz* was launched (in December 1974), they got Protima Bedi to streak on the same beach for their inaugural issue. Controversy erupted and the issue was a success. That's what you needed to do to upstage *Stardust* in its prime!

till the stars lost interest. Raj Kapoor sued the magazine after it reviewed his forthcoming film as 'Satyam Shivam Boredom', and he wasn't the only one. Years later, stars like Shah Rukh Khan and Anupam Kher have created a ruckus at the Stardust office and beat up one of their journalists respectively. Well into the 1990s and 2000s, *Stardust* was in the news for featuring a topless Mamta Kulkarni on their cover (for which she was fined) and for breaking the news of Aamir Khan's love child with a British journalist (for which the magazine was not sued).

During the Emergency, their copy was heavily censored – especially content related to Amitabh Bachchan. So they decided to stop covering him altogether. It takes a special brand of chutzpah for a film magazine to stop covering the industry's biggest star, but they managed just fine with their other scandals. In a meeting, V.C. Shukla – then in-charge of the information and broadcasting ministry – told Shobhaa De, 'We could hang you in a public square for what you are writing in *Stardust*.' Yup, they were that scandalous, dahlings!

Rajesh Khanna marries Dimple Kapadia

There was a buzz about Dimple. Raj Kapoor's *Bobby*, with her in the lead, was scheduled to release later that year and the industry was agog with speculation. Film-makers were falling over themselves to sign her on without even watching her first film. She was being offered Rs 5 lakh per film – the highest rate for heroines at that time. And in the midst of this, she went to Ahmedabad for a show on a chartered flight. One of her co-passengers was the reigning superstar, Rajesh Khanna. He was silent through the entire flight, till it was time to land. He then turned to Dimple and simply asked her if she would marry him. Seven days later, they were married. Dimple Kapadia gave up her chance to become a top heroine of the 1970s when – at not even sixteen years of age – she said yes to the 31-year-old man they called 'The Phenomenon'. *The Illustrated Weekly of India* simply called it the 'motion picture event of the year'.

It was as whirlwind a courtship as it could get. About a week after the airborne proposal, 6,000 guests – including all the biggest stars – attended their evening reception at Hotel Horizon in Juhu after the wedding was conducted at Dimple's father's bungalow as per Arya Samaj rites. After the wedding, Dimple had to return to the sets of *Bobby*, and her newly applied mehndi had to be hidden during filming. They went to Europe for their honeymoon in June and celebrated Dimple's sixteenth birthday with a party at the Hilton in London. Amitabh and Jaya Bachchan were also in London for their honeymoon at the time (having married just a few days after *Zanjeer* was declared a massive hit), and were the only guests from the film industry at the party.

It is said that the wedding was 'arranged' to boost Rajesh Khanna's flagging career and the prospects of Dimple Kapadia's debut film. If it was indeed that, the strategy was successful. *Bobby* was the biggest hit of the year, pulling Raj Kapoor out of the debts he had slid into after *Mera Naam Joker*. Rajesh Khanna temporarily fought back the challenge to his stardom with *Daag* and *Namak Haraam*. It didn't end well though…

Rajesh Khanna's career declined inexorably with the advent of Amitabh Bachchan as the Angry Young Man. Dimple Kapadia couldn't reconcile with the opportunities she had lost with the obviously uncomfortable marriage she had walked into. And the couple separated less than a decade later.

The short run-up to the wedding pre-empted any thoughts of problems that could arise from a May–December union. Dimple was taken up with the thought of marrying the most popular man in the country, while Rajesh was trying to get back at his long-standing lover, Anju Mahendru. Their love story had soured to the extent that Anju had threatened to have Rajesh thrown out by her security if he came to her house. Rajesh Khanna decided to rub it in by diverting his wedding procession to go in front of her house. That was probably the most thought-through gesture of the industry's most-anticipated wedding.

Zanjeer releases

A police officer looks a gangster in the eye and says, *'Jab tak baithne ko na kaha jaye, sharafat se khade raho. Yeh* police station *hai. Tumhare baap ka ghar nahin.'* It shocked the audience into silence. And the silence was finally broken when someone exclaimed, *'Arre, baap re baap'* in the theatre – a response never seen before in Hindi cinema.

Zanjeer introduced the Angry Young Man to audiences of Hindi cinema. After three decades of singing songs around trees and suffering in silence against injustices, the hero finally hit back. And his simmering rage reflected the mood of the nation. The crime, the corruption, the unemployment, the illegal trade of medicines and food had continued unabated since

Independence, and people were tired of the escapist fantasies of the 1960s. *Zanjeer*'s Amitabh Bachchan was the vigilante people were looking for.

Zanjeer also introduced Salim–Javed as the prime movers of the film industry for the next decade. It was not the first movie they co-wrote, but their first independent credit, and they participated actively by providing a complete script, recommending the cast (including the lead actor) and promoting themselves aggressively. On the eve of *Zanjeer*'s release, Salim–Javed realized that producer–director Prakash Mehra had not included their names in the posters. This was a massive blow to them because they were looking for credit as much as they were looking for money. They hired a painter and gave him a stencil of 'Written by Salim–Javed', which was used to paint their names on every poster of *Zanjeer* all over Bombay. *Zanjeer* had an untested actor, a relatively new director (who was producing for the first time) and unknown writers. But the writing duo ensured that they didn't go unnoticed in the success of the film. For the next ten years.

Most significantly for Hindi cinema, *Zanjeer* was the film that 'introduced' Amitabh Bachchan. A lanky newcomer, who had brooding eyes, had seemed wholly unsuited to the romance and musical formula that was the staple then. He had a few good

performances under his belt, but nothing to set the box office on fire. He was signed on for *Zanjeer* only after nearly the entire roster of heroes (from Dilip Kumar to Dev Anand to Raj Kumar to Dharmendra to even Navin Nischol) had turned down the film, and Salim–Javed kept on recommending him incessantly. When the film released, he was the third biggest draw of the film – after Pran and Jaya Bhaduri (who was a big star and Amitabh's girlfriend). After the film released, he was on the first page of every single trade magazine in the country, and people could not stop gushing. The entire trade had warned Prakash Mehra from taking him on and he managed to prove every one of his detractors wrong. Over the next five decades, Amitabh Bachchan would become a megastar, a member of Parliament, the Star of the Millennium and India's first social media celebrity. He arrived with *Zanjeer*. Or, as he introduced himself to the villain with a menacing confidence: '*Teja, main aa gaya hoon.*'

Government bans *Aandhi*

'Indira Gandhi on the screen': The poster for *Aandhi* declared. And if there was any doubt, there was a hand-drawn portrait of Indira Gandhi, then the country's prime minister, in between two stills of the film's lead stars – Suchitra Sen and Sanjeev Kumar. It was with this kind of publicity that Gulzar's political drama released, and all of India was convinced that it was based on the life of Indira Gandhi.

The similarities were striking. A strong-willed woman leaves her husband to make a career in politics. With the help of an influential father, she rises very fast. As she ages, her hair has a distinctive streak of white. She walks briskly, her gait reflecting her no-nonsense attitude. There were other similarities too. The film's hero, Sanjeev Kumar, is a hotelier – Feroze Gandhi too ran a hotel in Allahabad. Like in the film, one of Indira Gandhi's rallies in Bhubaneshwar was pelted with stones. Even the large-dialled watch Suchitra Sen wore in the film was reminiscent of the prime minister's personal style.

Writer–director Gulzar has clarified multiple times that the script he wrote wasn't based on her life, though the mannerisms were – because she was the most visible woman politician in the country then. Whether he was influenced by a real-life politician, consciously or subconsciously, while writing a fictional story, should be irrelevant to a discussion about artistic freedom. But, oh darling, *yeh hai* India!

Prior to the film's release, the then minister for information and broadcasting – Inder Kumar Gujral – had watched, liked and approved the film. *Aandhi* released in February 1975, and had a long theatrical run. Its distributors ran campaigns alluding to the film being Indira Gandhi's biopic and, while that ruffled feathers, no action was taken. However, a flurry of things happened in June 1975. During the bitterly fought assembly elections in Gujarat, the opposition used scenes from *Aandhi*, which showed Suchitra Sen smoking and drinking, to attack the prime minister. The anti-incumbency wave sweeping the country meant that Congress lost power in Gujarat for the first time since

Independence. By 26 June, Emergency had been imposed in the country and, using the sweeping powers available to it now, the Congress government at the Centre banned *Aandhi* five months after its release. The film was taken off theatres and posters were ordered to be removed.

If the ban was draconian, the solution was elegance personified. Gulzar – who was attending the Moscow Film Festival showcasing *Aandhi* – came back to India and, after some hectic parleying, decided to shoot a scene in which Suchitra Sen stands in front of a photograph of Indira Gandhi and declares, '*Yehi toh mere* ideal *hain.*' Thus, conclusively proving that she wasn't the person herself. The film was back in theatres and the country moved on to bigger atrocities brought about by the Emergency.

Doordarshan airs *Bobby*

At 10 p.m. on 5 February 1977 – a Saturday – an announcement was made on Doordarshan that the superhit film *Bobby* would be screened as the 'Sunday film' – a weekly routine for Indian television viewers. The originally planned *Waqt* was to be replaced by *Bobby*. Not only that, the time of telecast was advanced as well, from the usual 6 p.m. to 5 p.m. – something never done before. What seemed like a bonanza for the large number of movie fans who depended on Doordarshan's Sunday film for their weekly fix was actually a devious mix of Bollywood and politics.

After 22 months of Emergency, Indira Gandhi announced elections in mid-January, at the Kumbh Mela being held at

Allahabad. The Opposition leaders, jailed this entire time, were released, but the political parties were in total disarray. When posters for an Opposition rally at Delhi's Ram Lila Maidan started appearing, no one seemed to believe that Indira Gandhi could lose. The rally – to kick off the election campaign – was to be held only six weeks before the polls. It was on the day of the rally that *Bobby* was slated to be aired on Doordarshan – ostensibly to keep people from attending the rally. If that was indeed the plan, it failed spectacularly, because a massive crowd not only spontaneously came for the rally, they cheered lustily and donated to the Opposition cause – thus kicking off a campaign that would end in a humiliating defeat for the Congress.

After the new government came to power, the Shah Commission was appointed to probe into the excesses during the Emergency. The 'conspiracy' of screening *Bobby* was duly investigated, and it was found out that the then minister of information and broadcasting, Vidya Charan Shukla, had himself asked the film to be aired instead of the scheduled *Waqt*, because 'social workers objected to [its] screening'. To further bolster this flimsy excuse, one reel of *Waqt* was damaged to render it useless for screening. It was further discovered that when the late-night announcement was made, Doordarshan was still not

in possession of a print of *Bobby*. An old, worn-out print was finally secured from a distributor's godown just an hour before the screening was scheduled.

This last-minute scramble is a ringing endorsement of the Indian political class's blatant misuse of power and Bollywood's enduring allure. Four years after it released, *Bobby* was still considered to be a watch prized enough to keep multitudes of people home. Raj Kapoor's direction, Dimple–Rishi's teenaged charm and Laxmikant–Pyarelal's music ultimately couldn't match the yearning for democracy and the stars of a different kind who spoke that day on a rickety stage at Ram Lila Maidan. One of them was a young firebrand leader called Atal Bihari Vajpayee, who defined the evening with a few lines he had composed at the spur of the moment:

'*Baad muddat ke mile hain deewane / Kehne sunne ko bahut hain afsane,*
Khuli hawa mein zara saans toh le lein / Kab tak rahegi azaadi kaun jaane?'

Sanjay Gandhi is sentenced over *Kissa Kursi Ka*

Elections are announced in Jan Gan Desh. A roadside peddler is set up as an idealistic leader by giving him '*netagiri ka* tonic, *inquilab ki goli aur samajwad ka* injection'. His party's slogan is '*gareebi hatao*' and their election symbol is a 'people's car'. The new leader wins the election through a lot of wheeling-dealing and with the help from a godman, Bhagwan Bhajneesh. He soon has money in Swiss bank accounts and a mistress called Ruby Diksana. A deaf and mute woman called Janata (played by Shabana Azmi) is literally wooed by the politician, but she eventually commits suicide over his unmet promises. The courts rule against the leader, but he jails Opposition leaders, calling it an Emergency. In the end, infighting between those in power ends their reign. Anyone half familiar with Indian politics of the 1970s would immediately realize how many potshots had been packed in the plot of *Kissa Kursi Ka* and why the ruling party was so cagey about it. The film, which used actual footage of anti-government protests, was made by Amrit Nahata – a disgruntled Congress MP who had joined Janata Party.

He had submitted the film to the Central Board of Film Certification for certification in April 1975 and it was decided over the next two months that it would be given a U certificate, subject to 24 cuts. However, the CBFC chairman blocked the film because of its anti-establishment stance, and the government seized the master prints. The film-maker approached the Supreme Court, which asked for a viewing of the film in order to decide.

What happened next was quite amazing and unprecedented. About two weeks before the Supreme Court viewing date, the minister for information and broadcasting – V.C. Shukla – carried the master print of the film in his official car to the prime minister's residence. It was received by Indira Gandhi's private secretary, R.K. Dhawan (who, incidentally, was also spoofed in the film). On Sanjay Gandhi's instructions, his security officers took the prints to his small car factory (which later went on to become Maruti) and destroyed it there. The remnants of the reels and cans were discovered later.

This chain of events unravelled when the security officers turned approvers in front of the Shah Commission, and a case was filed against Sanjay Gandhi and V.C. Shukla. Even with the Janata Party in power, it took the sessions court two years to pronounce the duo as guilty. But it was quite momentous that two of the country's most powerful people felt threatened enough by a badly made film to ensure its destruction, and that they were convicted for it!

However, nothing came out of it. Sanjay Gandhi and V.C. Shukla's sentences were overturned when Janata Party was voted out of power. Amrit Nahata had remade the film and released it in 1978, by which time the public anger against the Congress had dissipated and the film sank without a trace. Over the years, *Kissa Kursi Ka* became a catchphrase for the devious struggles of power that keep happening even today. And for nearly sending a prime minister's son to jail.

Dilawar Khan marries Ayesha Bi

The nikahnama stated that Dilawar Khan Kewal Krishna (probably the most secular name ever!) accepted Ayesha Bi R. Chakravarthy as his wife… At a mehr of ₹1,11,000 in the presence of two legal witnesses, with the nikah being solemnized by Maulana Qazi Abu Talha Misbahi Faizabadi. The groom's address was noted as Plot No. 22, Road No. 11, J.V.P.D. Scheme, Juhu, Mumbai. The nikah between two seemingly affluent people with slightly unusual names had a simple explanation to it. It was the culmination of one of Bollywood's most enduring love stories – Dharmendra and Hema Malini.

The subterfuge was necessary to bypass the (seemingly small) problem of Dharmendra already being married. Islam, which allowed multiple marriages as per its personal laws, was the solution. And they lived happily ever after.

The Dharmendra–Hema Malini love story had all the ingredients of the filmi love stories we grew up on a steady diet of. Hema Malini felt attracted to Dharmendra right from the beginning, but didn't see a future with a married man. In the meantime, she had other suitors in the form of Sanjeev Kumar and Jeetendra – not to mention the 'eligible bachelors' whose photos her parents were plying her with. The Jeetendra affair extended to the point of him landing up in Madras (now Chennai) with his parents in tow to get married (in 1974). The news was broken by an evening paper, and Dharmendra did what any self-respecting Hindi film hero would do. He also turned up in Madras – with Shobha (then Jeetendra's girlfriend and now his wife) in tow. The resultant chaos led to the wedding getting scuttled. Jeetendra and Hema maintained a cordial relationship, despite a possessive Dharmendra breathing down their neck. The central tension of the love story was ultimately 'resolved' through the nikah in 1979, and that paved the way for their formal wedding in the Tamil Iyengar tradition (which happened on 2 May 1980). And they lived happily ever after.

A woman rebelling against her parents for love. A man breaking the laws of society for love. If this were a film, it would have been a blockbuster. But real life is a lot more prosaic. Dharmendra filed his nomination to fight the Lok Sabha elections in 2004, as a candidate for Bharatiya Janata Party. His opponents promptly pointed out that he had missed mentioning his second wife in his nomination, not to mention his conversion to Islam. Dharmendra brazened it out and ignored the charges, which didn't matter to his voters either, because he won the poll quite convincingly. Hema Malini faced similar charges during her campaigns, but they didn't seem to make any difference to her political career either. And they lived happily ever after.

Sanjay Khan assaults Zeenat Aman

Zeenat Aman was shooting for *Insaf ka Tarazu* in Lonavla when she received a call from Sanjay Khan. Over a tumultuous 30-minute call, he asked her to allot dates to reshoot a small portion of a song in his home production, *Abdullah*. When she refused, he abused her and then accused her of having affairs with her co-stars. A distraught Zeenat – still in love with Sanjay – took a break from the shooting and returned to Bombay to reason with Khan. She reached Taj Mahal Hotel where Sanjay Khan was attending a private party. A drunk Sanjay taunted her and – in a shocking act that went on for a while – started beating her up mercilessly, egged on by his wife, Zarine Khan. Other guests looked on till a hotel steward finally rescued Zeenat and escorted her to the car. Her face was covered with bruises; she was bleeding from her nose and her lips were badly cut when she staggered out of the hotel.

This was not just a producer–actor relationship gone sour. Zeenat Aman had famously said about Sanjay Khan, 'I love this man… I will back his every move and I will make him a king one day.' And they had secretly gotten married about a year back during a Jaisalmer shooting schedule of *Abdullah*. Industry gossip claimed that Sanjay Khan married Zeenat Aman to keep her fully engaged in the film, and decided to dump her once the film was complete. Whatever be the reason for the grotesque violence, it had a devastating impact on the actor. One of her eyes suffered permanent damage, seriously impacting her career as a leading lady. The mental trauma of the public humiliation – estimated by her doctors – took several months to heal. And despite all this, nothing really happened, because the film industry just looked the other way. And Zeenat Aman didn't report the incident to the police either.

Shobhaa De, then editor of *Stardust*, wrote: 'It remains one of the most sordid and shocking incidents in the history of Bollywood. Had it occurred in today's times, it would have made it to the front pages of our dailies. And [Sanjay] would have been jailed for abuse and assault.' While her sentiment about the crime is right, she couldn't be more wrong on the assessment of the punishment. In 2000, Bollywood's number one actress Aishwarya Rai accepted her Filmfare Best Actress trophy (for *Hum Dil De Chuke Sanam*) with a cast on one arm and dark glasses covering her face, presumably to hide a black eye. While she said on stage the injuries were due to a fall, she confessed in an explosive interview nearly three years later, 'There were times when Salman [Khan] got physical with me, luckily without leaving any marks. And I would go to work as if nothing had happened.' She ended her relationship with Salman, but filed no charges against him.

For several decades, and even now, rumours continue to swirl among Bollywood insiders about other high-profile cases of domestic violence and physical abuse. But nothing comes out of it. Ever.

Kamal Haasan debuts in Hindi

What do you call a debutant who has been in films for more than two decades, starting as a child actor and going on to become a star? What if the debutant has been in more than 110 films previously? This was Kamal Haasan's stature when he debuted in Bollywood with *Ek Duuje Ke Liye,* after a thriving career in all four South Indian film industries.

Kamal was the first South Indian male star to make it big in Hindi cinema – since the only imports from the South were heroines before this. South Indian actors often have a thick accent, which was turned into an advantage by making it a plot point of *Ek Duuje Ke Liye.* A Tamil boy and a North Indian girl fall in love, despite stiff parental opposition and major cultural differences. It was the remake of a Telugu film starring Kamal, which promptly became the second-biggest hit of the year,[8] after the Amitabh Bachchan–starrer *Laawaris*. The Hindi film audience took an instant liking for the slightly bewildered 'Madrasi' trying to romance a North Indian girl with his stilted Hindi. His unconventional looks – totally unlike the Hindi film he-man until then – didn't matter, thanks to his understated but very effective acting. Kamal also turned out to be a fantastic dancer, having trained in Bharatanatyam in his teens. All this led to him being offered a massive roster of 'big' films at fees that made him second only to Amitabh Bachchan. He was nominated for Filmfare's Best Actor award for *Ek Duuje Ke Liye* and *Sadma*, before winning it for *Saagar*. In a record of sorts, he was nominated as both Best Actor and Best Supporting Actor for *Saagar*, stealing the thunder from the lead pair – Dimple Kapadia and Rishi Kapoor (who were reuniting after *Bobby*). And it wasn't only his acting prowess that had audiences eating out of his hand. Kamal's second Hindi film was *Sanam Teri Kasam*, a musical extravaganza with a killer soundtrack. He also acted in multi-starrers like *Raj Tilak* and *Geraftaar* in meaty roles.

8. It was an unlikely success. The film's distributor in Bombay, Gulshan Rai, was not very confident himself, because he had distributed Bengali superstar Uttam Kumar's Hindi debut *Chhoti Si Mulaqat* in the past, and that had flopped despite great music and good performances.

Kamal Haasan's Hindi debut also paved the way for another major star in another major hit – Rajinikanth in *Andhaa Kaanoon.* (*Ek Duuje Ke Liye* also saw playback singer S.P. Balasubrahmanyam debuting in Hindi, and he remained popular for a very long time in Bollywood.)

Despite very solid starts, neither Kamal Haasan nor Rajinikanth created a major body of work in Bollywood. The majority of their films didn't even come close to their larger-than-life image in the South, relegating them to clichéd roles or insignificant parts. Delays in Bollywood productions meant they couldn't split time efficiently between Bombay and Madras, getting stuck in a few projects. There were also rumours that the big guns of Bombay kept them out of some big productions, fearing a Southern takeover of the industry ('Why the Bombay heroes hate Kamal's guts' ran one film magazine headline).

Eventually, Kamal[9] and Rajini went back to their mega-stardom in the South, and made occasional sorties through guest appearances, remakes and dubbed versions. And Bollywood remained poorer for that.

9. Kamal Haasan was active in Hindi cinema for only four years in the 1980s. His last film in that stint was *Dekha Pyar Tumhara* (also opposite Rati Agnihotri), before he returned, many years later, with his bilingual directorial ventures in the late 1990s.

Salim and Javed split

'I was thinking that maybe we should work separately,' Javed Akhtar had said at the end of a day's work. Salim Khan was at Javed's Juhu home, where they brainstormed, wrote and plotted how to take over the world. Despite some recent friction they'd experienced, Salim was taken aback. After digesting the words, Salim replied that Javed would have taken such a decision only after giving it considerable thought and nothing was likely to change his mind. As he began to walk towards his car, Javed also started walking to see him off. 'I am old enough to take care of myself,' Salim said, and sent him back. And Salim–Javed went their separate ways.

Salim Khan and Javed Akhtar, Hindi cinema's most successful screenwriters, had endured for slightly more than a decade in a partnership in which they wrote films that went on to become all-time classics, gamechangers, trendsetters, blockbusters, with just one flop under their belt. From being paid a pittance (₹10,000) for their first film as a duo (*Haathi Mere Saathi*), they commanded a price of ₹12.5 lakhs for *Dostana,* which was more than what Amitabh Bachchan was paid for the film. This was poetic justice in two ways. Firstly, they were credited with creating Hindi cinema's biggest star through their scripts – *Zanjeer, Deewaar, Don, Trishul, Kaala Patthar* – that defined his Angry Young Man persona. Secondly, the writer was largely unimportant – underpaid and uncredited – in the Hindi film industry, and Salim–Javed changed that equation with their talent, confidence and flamboyance.

The reasons for their split have been endlessly speculated. It has been reported that they fell out over Amitabh Bachchan's refusal to act in their script about an invisible man, which would later become *Mr India.* It has also been reported that Javed wanted to write songs under their joint moniker, but Salim wasn't okay with putting his name on lyrics that he had not contributed to. Irrespective of the reason, it was unanimously agreed that the split was premature and changed the very direction of the 1980s. In their solo avatars, Salim and Javed did a redux of Angry Young Man, bringing a timely twist to the character. Salim Khan wrote Sanjay Dutt in *Naam* and Amitabh Bachchan in *Akayla*. Javed Akhtar wrote Sunny Deol in *Arjun* and *Dacait*, Anil Kapoor in *Meri Jung* and *Mashaal*. Separately, they wrote a new avatar of the character and, while the films were very successful, they didn't quite have the magic of the originals. After being active through most of the 1980s, Salim retired from the film world and Javed concentrated almost entirely on writing lyrics.

But what was the impact of their split really? Who knew it best? Talking about Salim–Javed's split, a leading film actor said, 'It's a shame that they parted ways; they were truly unbeatable. Quite often, the media would conjecture what will happen to Amitabh Bachchan without Salim–Javed? Really, once they separated I couldn't ever get that kind of intensity again; that power was missing.' The man who said this was, yes, Amitabh Bachchan.

Amitabh Bachchan lives

Jaya Bachchan walked barefoot from Breach Candy Hospital to Siddhi Vinayak temple and back, as a major operation was being performed on her husband – probably India's most well-known person then. Amitabh Bachchan had gone into a coma and, at 9 p.m., he was declared clinically dead. When she was brought into the room for one last look, she noticed his little toe twitching and alerted the doctors. Dr Farokh Udwadia, the doctor leading the medical team, ordered cortisone injections till Bachchan revived. And indeed, he was resurrected – in what seemed like a scene from the movies he starred in. And the hero this time was Dr Udwadia, who went home that night and asked his mother to pray for his patient. And to take his mind off things, he played the violin till 3 a.m. in the morning. It was as filmi as it could get.

A mistimed punch from Puneet Issar on the sets of *Coolie* had caused Bachchan's intestine to rupture, leading to a flood of other complications. After one preliminary operation in Bangalore, he was shifted to Breach Candy and a second surgery was attempted on 2 August. His clinical death and subsequent revival were as much tales of medical excellence as they were of a nation's faith. When the superstar was down, the entire country prayed as one. The prime minister, Indira Gandhi, flew down to see him. People undertook the strictest of penances. One young man walked backwards all the way from Baroda to Bombay. An erstwhile black marketer stood at the hospital gates every day to hand over a single rose for the man on whose movie tickets he had made his fortune. M.F. Husain painted a picture of Hanuman bringing back the famous sanjeevani herb, while Bal Thackeray made a cartoon about Bachchan beating back Yamraj, the god of death.

Just a couple of years before this accident, Bachchan was called the 'One Man Industry' by a leading magazine. The many milestones marking his already gigantic stardom were repeated in the media many times during his hospital stay. Bachchan's excruciating recovery was also a period of extended communion with his legion of fans. Crowds started assembling outside his house in Juhu. After his recovery, the actor started coming out to thank them. And for the last four decades, the Sunday darshan in front of Bachchan's house has become a tradition – a display of devotion quite unmatched in terms of both numbers and durability.

Amitabh Bachchan was in the hospital for two months. When he was fit enough to get up, he immediately fell to the ground because the long period of inaction had turned his legs rubbery. He could have left the hospital in a wheelchair, but he decided – much like the heroes he played – that he had come to the hospital on a stretcher and would leave on his feet. For several sleepless nights, he practised walking – going from the bed to the end of the room and back. And finally, Amitabh Bachchan walked out of Breach Candy Hospital one day in September. Cloth banners all over the city proclaimed, 'God is great. Amitabh is back.' Amitabh was not only back, he was now god.

Qayamat Se Qayamat Tak releases

'Who's Aamir Khan? Ask the girls next door.'

The publicity campaign of *Qayamat Se Qayamat Tak* started with a teaser, usually not the best way to promote a newcomer. It was produced by Nasir Hussain, when the director was at a career low, confused about how to navigate the Hindi film industry of the 1980s. Action was the order of the day, romance was just a tick mark and music was no longer the selling point. Hussain looked at his next generation – son Mansoor and nephew Aamir – to revive his faltering banner. They started with a script idea that was called – in typical old Bollywood fashion – *Nafrat Ke Waaris*. And ended up making – what film historian Gautam Chintamani calls – 'the film that revived Hindi cinema'.

Qayamat Se Qayamat Tak was Mansoor Khan's directorial debut, but the clarity of his vision belied his newcomer status. He declined his father's long-time favourite Rahul Dev Burman as the composer, saying that he would never be able to give feedback freely to the senior 'Pancham Uncle'. He brought in rank newcomers Anand–Milind to compose the music, but had septuagenarian Majrooh Sultanpuri write the lyrics. The script was jointly written by the father–son duo, often clashing over old-school and newer values. But Mansoor Khan's biggest battle was to convince his producer-father to have a tragic ending for the film. Ever since Nasir Hussain's *Baharon Ke Sapne* had flopped, the maker had developed a phobia for sad endings. He begged his son to shoot a happy ending as well, though Mansoor Khan threatened that he wouldn't allow his name to be used if the film had a happy ending. Older audiences preferred the happy ending, but youngsters loved the sad one. The deadlock was finally broken by veteran writer Rahi Masoom Reza, whom Hussain considered to be the wisest man in the industry. Reza told him, 'If you have the happy ending, the film will do well and make a lot of money. But the film will never become a classic.'

And a classic it did become. Towards the end of the 1980s, Hindi cinema was still finding different ways to rehash the 'Angry Young Man' formula from 15 years ago. *Qayamat Se Qayamat Tak* was the first romantic blockbuster after ages – with a fresh take on the classic *Romeo and Juliet* plot. The lead players – Aamir Khan and Juhi Chawla – were nothing like the heroes and heroines who were ruling the roost then. And the music was a breath of fresh air – traditional melodies, but in a very modern style. The music was picked up by Super Cassettes, which would soon become a musical powerhouse on the back of several superhit soundtracks. After *Qayamat Se Qayamat Tak* came a slew of romantic hits – Yash Chopra's *Chandni*, Sooraj Barjatya's *Maine Pyar Kiya*. And romance was once again the flavour of the season, bringing family audiences back to the theatres and taking the first step towards making Hindi cinema cool again. It was also the first Hindi film to have a hip acronym, and the girls next door couldn't get enough of QS Cutie (a play on QT).

Sanjay Dutt is arrested

Sanjay Dutt's career is dotted with several abysmally bad films that he needn't have done. However, nothing was more avoidable – from his perspective – as two forgettable films called *Yalgaar* and *Sanam*. During the shooting of *Yalgaar* in Dubai, Sanjay was introduced to Dawood Ibrahim and became pally with the gangster's younger brother, Anis. When he signed *Sanam*, he got in touch with producers Hanif–Samir, who were interrogated for their involvement in the Bombay blasts of 1993. Anis Ibrahim had sold Sanjay Dutt an AK-56 gun. And Hanif–Samir squealed to the police about this.

When Hanif–Samir's testimony was leaked to the press, Sanjay was shooting for *Aatish* in Mauritius. He landed in

Bombay about a week later, and was immediately whisked away for interrogation at 2.15 a.m. He was arrested later that day, and thus, started a trial that would continue for more than 20 years.

The story started with the Bombay riots of December 1992, which turned the city into a communal tinderbox. Principled Congress leader Sunil Dutt resigned as an MP to protest his own government's inability to control the riots, and created powerful enemies within his party. When Sanjay confessed to buying a gun for self-defence, he claimed that it was due to the multiple death threats he was receiving from right-wing Hindu parties. So, when the gun was finally discovered in his friend's residence (where they had melted it down), he and his father were friendless in politics. Sanjay didn't get bail for 15 months and, ironically, it was Congress' arch-rival – and Shiv Sena supremo – Bal Thackeray who lobbied to get him released. As quid pro quo, Sunil Dutt gave up his stronghold constituency, Bombay North West, which Shiv Sena won in the next two elections.

It was a rollercoaster for Sanjay on the professional and personal front. His relationship with Madhuri Dixit ended. *Khalnayak*, with him in the title role, did phenomenal business, but further blurred the lines between the reel and the real. His films were forced off several theatres across the country, but the mayhem settled down when the due process of law took over.

He was sentenced in 2013 and the ordeal finally ended in 2016, when he completed his jail term.

Sanjay Dutt's arrest was – and still is – Bollywood's most high-profile brush with the law. There have been many instances of top stars – most notably, Salman Khan – being embroiled in criminal cases, but none of them came close to being accused in a terrorism case. Sanjay Dutt's psychiatric profile says that he shows 'self-destructive traits ... narcissism ... immaturity'. He had a childish fascination for guns, which sparked this whole issue, but his family – one of Bollywood's most respected – fought tooth and nail against the terror charges. It was a small victory for them when Sanjay was finally convicted for possession of weapons, but was acquitted of charges related to the Bombay blasts. Sanjay Dutt may have been foolish, but he wasn't a terrorist.

David Dhawan and Govinda's *Aankhen* releases

A Bollywood producer of the 1990s once said, 'The problem with Govinda is that he just can't say no. Thank god he's not a woman.' This tongue-in-cheek comment is accurate, though, because of his desire to become a top star and his inability to say no, Govinda acted in more than 50 nondescript movies in just the first six years of his Bollywood career. While many of these films made money for their producers and built a reputation for Govinda, he was nowhere close to being a superstar. Till he came across David Dhawan.

David Dhawan and Govinda had worked in a couple of moderately successful films before their first big hit – *Shola Aur Shabnam*, a typical potboiler with Govinda going from a carefree cadet to an avenging angel. And then they hit upon the formula that would make them rule the 1990s, to the utter delight of their producers, and exasperation of critics and the moral police. The formula included Govinda's exuberant dancing, his brilliant comic timing, a couple of double-meaning songs (complete with pelvic thrusts) and a largeish supporting cast in a zany plot. And their first monster hit, *Aankhen,* executed this playbook perfectly.

Two wastrels (Govinda and Chunky Pandey) stumble upon a plot to exchange the chief minister with a body double. While they are on the run from the gang organizing the switch, one more Govinda and one more Kader Khan pop up. If that wasn't enough, there's a stock market scam, a monkey, a whole list of practical jokes and – what would soon be a Dhawan–Govinda trademark – songs that walked the thin line between saucy and indecent. Women's groups were up in arms as one song ('*Lal dupatta wali*') became some sort of a roadside harassers' anthem, while another ('*Angna mein baba, duware pe maa*') was bolstered by hiked-up *ghagras* and incredibly aggressive pelvic thrusts.

Aankhen went on to become the biggest hit of 1993, starting a trend that would last the better part of the decade. David Dhawan and Govinda had their individual successes, but their combination was a different level of crazy. Right after *Aankhen* – in successive years – came *Raja Babu, Coolie No. 1* and *Saajan*

Chale Sasural, Hero No. 1, Deewana Mastana and *Bade Miyan Chote Miyan*, all of which were huge hits. In the 1990s, they were compared with other legendary partnerships, such as Shakti Samanta–Rajesh Khanna and Manmohan Desai–Amitabh Bachchan.

There's a lot to criticize in the David Dhawan–Govinda films. The stories were often regressive, the humour crass and the acting loud. But what they did almost perfectly was to cater to the guilty pleasures of the masses, which slowly reached the so-called sophisticated strata. In 1993, the swish set were sniggering at '*Angna mein baba*', but by 1999, all the discos – and Ramlila grounds – in the country were dancing to '*Kisi disco mein jaaye*'. Sure, some people were offended, but as they put it, '*Tujhe mirchi lagi toh main kya karoon?*'

Phir Teri Kahani Yaad Aayee premieres on Zee TV

Mahesh Bhatt's father was not formally married to his mother, creating a stigma of illegitimacy around his childhood. As a young and upcoming director, he had an affair with Parveen Babi, but he abandoned her, unable to cope with her mental illnesses. These two experiences became thematic obsessions for him, and he made a series of 'autobiographical films' – beginning with *Arth*.

The next film in this 'series' was *Janam*, starring Kumar Gaurav as a young director in search of parental identity and approval. What was unusual, though, was the medium. In 1985, *Janam* aired on Doordarshan as a telefilm, and Bhatt remembers that the nightly national news bulletin was delayed by 14 whole minutes till the film got over. In 1989, Bhatt again used telefilm as a medium to make *Daddy* – marking the debut of his daughter Pooja – also a tale of estranged parenthood.

In 1991, satellite television was introduced in the country, with several Indian and international channels beginning to air. From the single state-run Doordarshan, there were now a dozen channels trying to create a glut of new content. Subhash Chandra, an Indian entrepreneur, made an offer to HutchVision (then owners of the Star TV channel) to start a joint-venture entertainment channel in India. When his proposal was rejected, he leased a transponder and launched the first Indian satellite channel, which soon became an entertainment empire. As Zee went from three hours of programming a day to six and then to 24, it commissioned a whole lot of content from a new pool of producers.

One of their game-changing moves to drive eyeballs was to commission a telefilm with a high-profile director, featuring a hot young cast and a superhit soundtrack. *Phir Teri Kahani Yaad Aayee* had Mahesh Bhatt straight off hits like *Dil Hai Ke Manta Nahin* and *Sadak*. Rahul Roy (of *Aashiqui* fame), Pooja Bhatt (of several-hit-films-with-her-father fame) and Pooja Bedi (of *Jo Jeeta Wohi Sikandar* fame) headlined the cast that was as hot as any major theatrical release. Anu Malik composed the music, which was a runaway bestseller. The story was vintage Mahesh Bhatt – about a film director falling in love with a mentally unstable woman and solving the attendant crises that follow.

What the telecast of the film did was to create unprecedented viewer interest in the cable television ecosystem. Thousands of households started subscribing to satellite TV, and advertisers followed suit. The premiere of *Phir Teri Kahani Yaad Aayee* had one of the heaviest advertisement densities on Indian television, going into breaks almost every quarter of an hour. With a bouquet of serials to back up this phenomenon, Zee TV was well and truly the first Indian entertainment powerhouse, which ruled airwaves during the 1990s. Star TV, which passed up the opportunity for a joint venture, changed ownership and upped the content ante in a different direction to fight Zee. It took them till 2000 to get there. Till then, it was Zee TV which showed the way of commissioning big-ticket 'original content' straight to television.

R.D. Burman passes away, his cult is born

In August 1994, an Indian-born artiste – Baljit Singh Sagoo – released a hit album, *Bollywood Flashback*, and became mainstream in Britain when one of the singles became the first Indian track to be played on BBC Radio 1. The single – from a film called *Yaadon Ki Baaraat* – was originally composed by an Indian who had passed away in January. His name was R.D. Burman. In a way, '*Chura liya*' was the perfect RD song to hit international airwaves through a remix, because he took its prelude from an international hit ('*If it's Tuesday, this must be Belgium*') and then made it his own through innovative orchestration and a lovely melody.

R.D. Burman's musical career of three decades was studded with many classic albums that included *Teesri Manzil, Kati Patang, Hare Rama Hare Krishna, Amar Prem, Yaadon Ki Baaraat, Aandhi, Ghar, Sanam Teri Kasam, Masoom, Saagar* and *Ijaazat,* indicating a range that was probably wider than that of any Hindi film music director. However, the late 1980s was a period of decline for him – big banners refusing to work with him, high-profile films flopping and his hits considered too niche. He was at a precariously low point in his career when Vidhu Vinod Chopra offered him *1942: A Love Story,* egged him to compose in the classic style and not bother with heavy-duty disco orchestration that was the flavour of the season. He delivered one of the most durable soundtracks of Hindi cinema and was awaiting his return to the top when he passed away rather abruptly.[10]

A combination of factors built the cult of RD, as we see it today. The music of *1942: A Love Story* released after his death, and was a runaway hit. He posthumously won (only) his third Filmfare award for Best Music. His position as the harbinger of

10. A New Year's Eve party was organized on the sets of *1942: A Love Story*. When R.D. Burman reached, '*Ek ladki ko dekha*' started playing and the entire party clapped for him, with fireworks going off. That was the only public adulation RD got for the film. He passed away four days later.

new trends in film music was further cemented when Filmfare instituted the R.D. Burman Award for New Music Talent in his honour (and the first winner was A.R. Rahman). The cult of RD got a boost when Sujoy Ghosh directed *Jhankaar Beats,* which was an unabashed tribute to Pancham – giving him the epithet 'Boss' and bringing music directors Vishal–Shekhar into the limelight. Another new film, *Dil Vil Pyar Vyar,* had its entire soundtrack comprised remixed songs of R.D. Burman, which was unprecedented in Hindi cinema. Beyond these major tributes, as discos and DJs proliferated in India, so did the remixes, and R.D. Burman was the undisputed king there. Balaji Vittal and Anirudha Bhattacharjee, in their seminal book, *R.D. Burman – The Man, The Music,* noted that DJs felt his music was best suited for mixing because most of his tracks are based on a 4x4 beat on which it is very easy to add on beats without much editing. RD's music was always considered modern and frivolous by purists, while youngsters loved them. With FM radio stations and music channels opening in large numbers in the 1990s, suddenly we could get his music at the push of a button and just couldn't have enough of it. It's just too sad that RD wasn't around to savour his success.

Hum Aapke Hain Koun..! releases

Sooraj Barjatya was at Bombay's Liberty Cinema where his *Hum Aapke Hain Koun..!* was running to packed shows. He noticed a gentleman with a medical drip attached to his arm in the theatre. He had come from Bombay Hospital (located almost next door) where he was being treated for high blood pressure. The patient told Barjatya that the film calmed him down far better than any treatment at the hospital. This is – in one story – the impact of *Hum Aapke Hain Koun..!*, the film which brought audiences back to the theatres. But it wasn't an accident. The Barjatyas, consummate film distributors themselves, planned it that way by taking a gamble like no other.

In the 1980s, the video boom had hit India. Films released on video the same time they did in theatres, and cinema footfall had dwindled. In this doomsday scenario, *Maine Pyar Kiya* had released to phenomenal business, bypassing the video boom. The film, starring a new lead pair and debutant director, had no takers on video, at least initially. It had also released in very few theatres to start with, and then kept adding shows and theatres as the craze built all over India. Thanks to the monster success of *Maine Pyar Kiya*, the anticipation for *Hum Aapke Hain Koun..!* was huge and the Barjatyas could have released it in hundreds of theatres. They chose to release it in only 30 cinemas across India, with just that one theatre – Liberty – in Bombay. This limited release was due to the strict conditions laid down by Barjatyas for cinemas to have high-quality audio systems, refurbished and clean interiors (including toilets). Theatres, which had fallen into disrepair due to low footfall during the video boom, agreed to make these changes to be able to release *Hum Aapke Hain Koun..!* Consequently, ticket prices were increased – breaching the three-figure mark in some centres – but audiences didn't seem to mind. Families booked entire rows for themselves and came to watch the film, creating a box-office tsunami. Without video cassettes, the shows became family outings. Because of the limited release, families hired whole buses to travel to nearby cities where the film was running. Grandparents came back to the theatre after decades. People finished one show and promptly went back to watch the next. And, of course, patients thought it was a viable treatment for hypertension!

Hum Aapke Hain Koun..! went on to become the biggest box-office hit – breaking *Sholay*'s 20-year-old record. It made superstars out of Madhuri Dixit, Salman Khan and Sooraj Barjatya. But that was not its only impact. *Hum Aapke Hain Koun..!* brought audiences back to the theatres – for good. Ticket prices climbed to a higher level and stayed there, forcing theatre owners to invest in and provide a high-quality experience. In the five years prior to the film (1989–1993), the biggest hits of the years collected an average of ₹12.2 crore. In the subsequent five years, the biggest hits collected an average of ₹44.2 crore, a fourfold jump. Fourteen songs, two weddings, a funeral and one Pomeranian changed Hindi cinema forever.

Gulshan Kumar is shot dead

Ram Gopal Varma was sitting with financier Jhamu Sughand when the latter got a phone call. He put down the phone, shocked, to announce that music mogul Gulshan Kumar had been shot dead. Gulshan Kumar had spoken to Sughand that very morning. Ram Gopal Varma wondered that if Kumar had woken up at 7 a.m., when would his killers have woken up? How would they have gotten ready? Varma had started shooting *Satya* (just the previous day) and this shooting made him reconsider the entire script – probably helping *Satya* reach the status of the definitive underworld film. The ordinary lives of gangsters seemed an obvious choice in hindsight because the underworld was literally all over Mumbai.

In a gruesome incident, Gulshan Kumar was killed by two contract killers just outside a temple, and he tried to take shelter in the nearby hutments, but people were too scared to let him in. He was killed because he refused to pay extortion money to the Dawood Ibrahim gang. Music director Nadeem Saifi was initially implicated in the killing, though he was acquitted for lack of evidence. Gulshan Kumar's murder was the most high-profile underworld killing, though several film stars had also been threatened and some even attacked around that period.

Bollywood's fascination with the underworld had started in the 1970s. *Deewaar* was said to be based on the life of mafia boss Haji Mastan. The don himself was infatuated with the movie world and even got married to a starlet. Bollywood's dalliances with the underworld increased in the 1980s during cricket matches at Sharjah and film shootings in UAE. Dawood Ibrahim, who was running his Indian empire from abroad, cultivated stars to feed his need for nostalgia, glamour and power. He and his extended gang were soon arbitrating film industry disputes and investing in films. Bollywood stoked their egos by inserting glamourized elements from their lives into films.

Sanjay Dutt's arrest in 1993 wasn't enough to deter Bollywood. Through the 1990s, Mafia money flowed freely into Bollywood – the most high-profile production being

Chori Chori Chupke Chupke starring Salman Khan, Rani Mukerji and Preity Zinta. The producer – Nazim Rizvi, an aide of Chhota Shakeel – was arrested and major Bollywood financier Bharat Shah followed soon after. Actresses like Mandakini and Monica Bedi had publicly known affairs with dons, while the 'underworld film' became a veritable genre in Bollywood. Even as the police was cracking down on producers with underground links, Bollywood was ingratiating itself to the dons. When Mahesh Manjrekar's *Vaastav* won a Filmfare award, its producer, Deepak Nikalje, was on stage with the director and star. This wouldn't have been of importance if Nikalje wasn't the brother of Rajan Nikalje, aka Chhota Rajan – a member of the Dawood Ibrahim's gang, who fell out with him and created his own gang – scratch that – company.

Kaun Banega Crorepati goes on air

Rupert Murdoch was in India to review plans for his newly acquired television channel, Star TV. The management had proposed betting big on Hindi language programming. One of the planned shows was the Hindi version of the international hit, *Who Wants to Be a Millionaire?* The idea was to make an ageing superstar the host and offer a maximum prize of 1 lakh rupees. *Kaun Banega Lakhpati?* was the show, because there's no Indian equivalent for 'million', the team explained. What's the next level in Indian numerals, Murdoch asked. Someone said it was a crore, or ten million. Make it that then, the media mogul advised.

Kaun Banega Crorepati upended several conventional notions about television watching in India – a bet Star TV made in order to catch up with the market leader, Zee TV. This included bringing back quizzing to prime-time television, which they did by roping in Siddharth Basu's company for content. Siddharth Basu had pioneered quizzing on Indian television with the exceedingly popular *Quiz Time*, and seemed the best candidate for making quiz geekery popular again.

The other ingredient in the mix was equally – if not more – potent: Bollywood. But this bet was riskier than everything else. Amitabh Bachchan was at the lowest ebb of his career, his Angry Young Man having fallen out of favour with the new-age audience – people weren't as angry with the system any more. His films in the previous few years had mostly been flops, and his newly floated company was facing bankruptcy. Getting such an actor was a risk and Bachchan himself wasn't sure of doing television. He visited the UK recording of the English show, questioned the production company and channel repeatedly before coming on board. Maybe his precarious financial condition and need for exposure also nudged him to take on the assignment (for an unheard-of fee that gave the Star TV bosses sleepless nights).

While Bachchan's commercial standing was low, his wide-ranging appeal,[11] bilingual eloquence and strong work ethic became assets to his new avatar as game show host. *Kaun Banega Crorepati* was launched with a publicity blitz, and it not only zoomed to the top of television ratings but became a benchmark of success for years to come. Suddenly, Bachchan became the nation's favourite uncle – albeit one who was helping you win big bucks. The effect of this new avatar rubbed off on his film roles as well, where he was often seen as the cool, older person. The success of the show also led him experimenting more, and Bachchan did some of his edgier roles in the early 2000s.

KBC became a national phenomenon, with top film stars regularly appearing as guests and fans finding a new channel to interact with Amitabh Bachchan – which is at least as strong a reason to appear on the show as the prize money. It pioneered the star-led game show genre on television and has remained the benchmark even now, 20 years later. And along with lines written by Salim–Javed and Kader Khan, one of Bachchan's most popular catchphrases became '*Deviyon aur sajjanon, aap sab ka bahut swagat hai iss adbhut khel mein... Jiska naam hai* Kaun Banega Crorepati*!*'

11. In June 2000, he became the first Indian actor to have a wax statue at Madame Tussauds.

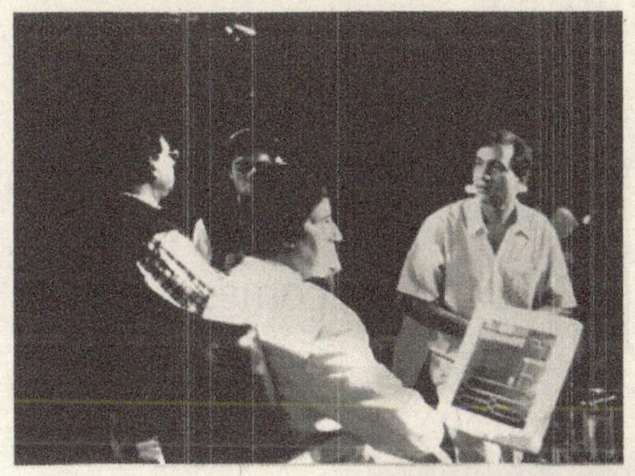

Siddhartha Basu directing Amitabh Bachchan on the sets of Kaun Banega Crorepati Season 1, on which Shoojit Sircar was also a director.

Image courtesy of Siddhartha Basu

Kabhi Khushi Kabhie Gham... becomes a hit

Yash Johar had bet his life's savings on his son's second film. And Karan Johar was a nervous wreck. He was convinced the film would flop, setting his family back to the days they struggled to catch a break. He spent the opening weekend agonizing over his expensive film. On 17 December – a Monday – a friend called him to Liberty Cinema to show him something. A little distance from Liberty, Karan got stuck in a traffic jam. He rolled down the window and asked a cop what the jam was for. The cop said, '*Woh* advance booking *ki line,* Kabhi Khushi Kabhie Gham... *ke liye...* Police *ko bulaya,* crowd control *ke liye.*' Karan Johar got out of the car and ran the rest of the way to see his biggest success for himself.

If you ask people their favourite film from 2001, the votes are likely to be split between *Lagaan* and *Dil Chahta Hai*. One was a rare Indian film to get nominated for an Oscar. The other was the harbinger of Bollywood abandoning kitsch and becoming cool. But neither was the year's top grosser.

Karan Johar had transformed the fortunes of his family production company – Dharma Productions – with his debut directorial venture, *Kuch Kuch Hota Hai*. For his second film, his doting father gave him a much bigger canvas to play with and the highest budget for a Hindi film till then – ₹50 crore. It started with the most dazzling star cast that was possible at the time. Karan Johar, due to his newfound reputation and Yash Johar's standing in the industry, managed to sign all six stars in one single day – going from one meeting to another. If the stars were big, the sets were even bigger. From Chandni Chowk to Egypt to London, the sweep of the film was massive. Whoever came to the sets went back awed. '*Yeh toh* Sholay *hai!*' they said. Karan Johar was so excited that he thought he was making *Mother India* (His words, not mine!).

What *Kabhi Khushi Kabhie Gham*... did was to create a genre that can possibly be called 'Yash Chopra-on-steroids'. (Karan Johar paid a subtle tribute to his guru by spelling the second *Kabhie* with an e, like Yash Chopra's *Kabhi Kabhie*).

He took Chopra's 1980s formula of emotion in a grand setting and turbocharged it. *K3G* showcased a Diwali, a Karwa Chauth and a national anthem rendition added to side plots involving cricket, song-and-dance and exotic locales (including but not restricted to British manors, the Pyramids of Giza and stadiums in the UK). It became the archetype of the grand Bollywood film. The international box-office had started becoming lucrative from the time *Dilwale Dulhania Le Jayenge* and Johar's previous film had done well abroad as well, but *K3G* eclipsed them all. The film debuted at No. 3 in UK box office, and its USA collection numbers were so unbelievably large that the reporting agency didn't report it (fearing errors). If they had released the numbers, *K3G* would have opened at No. 10 in North America. At the Indian box office, the opening week collection was 70 per cent more than the previous record. Karan Johar was soon to become a mini-ecosystem within Bollywood. And it all started when he became the darling of the box-office.

Whizkid director Karan Johar's close relationship with stars is instrumental in getting never-before multi-starrer casts for his films.

Under license by Dharma Productions Private Limited

No Man's Land wins an Oscar for Best Foreign Language Film

Sharon Stone and John Travolta did a little jig as they made their way to the on-stage microphone at Hollywood's Kodak Theatre. They gave short introductions of the countries and languages that were the five nominees for the Best Foreign Language Film at the 74th Academy Awards. And then Travolta broke a billion hearts by reading out Bosnia and Herzegovina's *No Man's Land* as the winner. As the director Danis Tanović made his way towards the stage, Indians could spot two familiar figures in *bandhgalas* clapping politely – the duo who had come closest to this prize in recent times.

Lagaan was only the third Indian film – after *Mother India* and *Salaam Bombay* – to have reached the final five nominees.

It is not a mean achievement to be in the top five out of 50-odd entries from across the world. This was largely possible because Aamir Khan brought his famously single-minded dedication to the Oscar campaign, which some people believe started as soon he began work on *Lagaan*. After its selection as the Indian entry, Aamir Khan and Ashutosh Gowariker camped in Los Angeles for months. Aamir used his film-star aura and a publicity agency to get interviewed by top entertainment publications like *The Hollywood Reporter*, *Variety* and *USA Today*. He got socialite Parmeshwar Godrej to speak to her friends like Steven Spielberg, Richard Gere and Ismail Merchant. Mira Nair, the previous nominee who also had *Monsoon Wedding* in the running, let go of her disappointment and wrote to her friends to watch *Lagaan*. The film's US distributor, Sony Pictures Classics, also pitched in with what seemed like a substantial budget of $2 million. Except the amount was dwarfed by the spends of Miramax to promote the global French hit, *Amélie*, also in the running. (Incidentally, it was the infamous Harvey Weinstein who started the custom of aggressively promoting films for Oscars.) The objective of the exercise is to ensure the nominee is seen by an anonymous group of about 750 members, who are eligible to vote for the Best Foreign Language Film award. Apart from them being anonymous, no direct canvassing or badgering is

allowed. Lobbying to them is a bit like throwing a dart in a dark room and moving ahead on a prayer... But hinging on a prayer is what *Lagaan* is all about!

So why didn't *Lagaan* win? Some felt that – at 222 minutes – it was way too long. Others felt that a cricket match in pre-Independence India was too alien a concept for Academy members. And some others felt the songs and dances were a bit over-the-top. Whatever be the reason for the loss, *Lagaan* is still the last Indian film to have reached the top five. We have often sent terribly incongruous films to the Oscars, while even the worthy contenders have blamed poor timing, lack of support, low budgets and dissipated campaigning to explain their exits.

Indians have won at the Oscars. But we are still waiting for India to win.

Koffee with Karan goes on air

In 2004, Karan Johar was the hottest producer in town. He was young and had a sharp sense of fashion. And thanks to him growing up among filmi kids, he had half the industry and their parents on speed dial. He was asked to host a television awards show on Star TV, which he laughed off as too downmarket, but offered to do a chat show for them instead. As the producers admit, the show is entirely his baby – from inviting, cajoling and getting the stars to show up, to the design, to even the type of questions being asked. And, of course, only he can get Shah Rukh Khan and Kajol to appear on the very first episode of an English chat show on a very niche English television channel.

'Spilling the beans while having a hot cuppa' was the original brief and in this gossip-crazy country, it's a formula hard to get wrong. *Koffee with Karan* was soon the highest-watched English show made in India, competing with the likes of *F.R.I.E.N.D.S.* The biggest names of Indian entertainment come on the show and reveal (or deny) their lives' deepest secrets – almost forgetting that there's a camera rolling. Only on *Koffee with Karan* can a Shah Rukh Khan joke about the gossip that he is in a relationship with Karan Johar and Salman Khan 'confess' that he's a virgin. It's here that two top actresses have suggested Ranbir Kapoor would be the best person to endorse a condom brand, while two international cricketers revealed how they pick up girls at a bar. And Kangana Ranaut split the industry in two by calling Karan Johar the 'flagbearer of nepotism'.

Koffee with Karan also has the impact that it gets noticed, and stormy discussions rage on the appropriateness of the pronouncements on the show. Rishi Kapoor swore never to work for Dharma Productions because of the potshots aimed at his son, Ranbir (and changed his mind as soon as Karan Johar apologized to him). Hardik Pandya and K.L. Rahul were briefly banned from international cricket for their misogynistic comments on the show. It was also the show on which Alia Bhatt failed to name the president of India, and inspired an avalanche of memes, jokes and a video that catapulted a comedy collective called All India Bakchod to national fame.

Over the years, *Koffee with Karan* had spawned an entire genre of catty, bitchy talk shows, but none has managed to match the star power of the original. Every major star and star kid have appeared on *Koffee,* desperate to get noticed by revealing salacious secrets about their lives and bitching about others, in order to win a 'Koffee Hamper' in the Rapid-Fire round. *Koffee with Karan* is also that plate-glass window into the lives of the rich and famous. When Alia Bhatt plays a game of 'Kill-Hookup-Marry' on the show, the silly game remains incomprehensible to most and it only explodes when her answer of 'Kill – Sushant' is made to look sinister after the actor passes away. For the right reasons or wrong, India cannot look away from *Koffee with Karan.*

Black Friday premiere is cancelled

Anurag Kashyap got his first suit stitched for the premiere of *Black Friday*. He had come down from his flat – ready to leave for the show – when his building's watchman asked him to go back up. He went upstairs, only to be told that the premiere was cancelled because the courts had stayed the film's release till the final verdict of the Bombay blasts' case was delivered. Kashyap went straight into his room and started drinking. And stayed in the suit for a month.

The making of *Black Friday* was thrilling. Anurag Kashyap was the proverbial 'struggler', who came to Bombay and found his first pay cheques writing scripts for TV shows. Less than 25 years old when he was selected to co-write *Satya*, he was seen as some sort of a wunderkind. But his ride into cinema was bumpy, to say the least. He made *Paanch* about a group of drifters who end up murdering a friend and go into a self-destructive spiral. The CBFC initially refused to certify the film because of its depiction of violence and drug abuse, and the foul language used. When the movie was finally cleared by the CBFC, the producer was not in a position to release it. *Black Friday* was conceived as a six-part mini-series (for news channel *Aaj Tak*) and Anurag Kashyap was only supposed to write the script. But *Aaj Tak* felt the subject was too controversial and backed out, when producer Mid-day Multimedia asked Kashyap to take over and direct the project as a film. *Black Friday* was made on a shoestring budget, at a time when the makers couldn't afford to even put up sets. This could have potentially stalled the project because the landscape of Mumbai had sprouted mobile phone towers and satellite TV hoardings since 1993, when the film was set. Kashyap and his crew resorted guerrilla film-making on the streets to make the film. Immediately after *Black Friday*, Kashyap also started shooting *Gulaal*, when producer Jhamu Sughand fell ill and the film got shelved. (He also shot an experimental film – *Allwyn Kalicharan* – with Anil Kapoor for six whole days before the star backed out.) With three-and-a-half films in various stages of uncertainty, the *Black*

Friday premiere getting cancelled was a terrible blow for the new director.

But it also marked a turning point that didn't let him fall into an abyss. *Black Friday* was extremely well-made – despite its shoestring budget – and became a benchmark in indie film-making. Danny Boyle named the 12-minute police chase through Dharavi as the inspiration for the opening scene of his Oscar-winning *Slumdog Millionaire*. *Black Friday* was shown at Locarno Film Festival, was a nominee for Best International Film and earned a name for the director in the festival circuit. All these – a low budget, edgy writing, technical finesse and international acclaim – would become a Kashyap trademark in his later films that turned his fortunes around, and established him as the godfather of arthouse cinema in India. But that was still four years away. Till then, there was a terrible hangover and a dirty suit to keep him company.

The Times of India runs P1 story on the Jessica Lall murder case

'No one killed Jessica' ran the banner headline on the *The Times of India*'s front page, the day after a Delhi trial court acquitted all the accused in the high-profile murder of model-turned-celebrity bartender Jessica Lal. And it became the only newspaper headline to become the title of a Hindi film.

Raj Kumar Gupta's movie portrayed the unfolding of the infamous case, though with some creative liberties taken and with thinly veiled fictional versions of the real characters. Rani Mukerji played a role based on the firebrand NDTV journalist Barkha Dutt, who ran a vocal campaign after the case ended at the trial court. Newsmagazine *Tehelka* wasn't featured in the film version, though it ran a sting campaign to expose the falsehoods of some of the witnesses who had turned hostile during the trial. The most high-profile and interesting debunking was actor Shayan Munshi's claim that he couldn't fully understand the proceedings because he didn't understand Hindi. The *Tehelka* team posed as talent scouts for a Hollywood production and managed to make him converse extensively in Hindi. Vidya Balan's portrayal of Sabrina Lal (the victim's sister) was understated, and she held the film together with a calm confidence.

The actual happenings after the trial court verdict were dramatic and made great material for a thriller. Civil society and the legal fraternity in Delhi rose as one against the verdict, which seemed to be influenced by the politically well-connected family of the main accused, Manu Sharma. Media outrage followed, with even international publications like *The New York Times* and *BBC* joining in. With no social media to speak of then, crowd mobilization happened through SMS and was surprisingly effective. The recently released *Rang De Basanti* inspired the way the protests were held, where people congregated at India Gate for a candlelight vigil against a corrupt government. An avalanche of messages – running into several lakhs – poured into television and print media houses, addressing the Supreme Court and president of India to intervene. The effect was felt very quickly. The Delhi Police agreed to reinvestigate the case and the prosecution appealed to the High Court for a review, which started with the court issuing fresh warrants for the accused just a month later. The High Court pronounced Manu Sharma guilty later that year. His father – a minister in the Haryana government – resigned under political pressure from his own party. The Supreme Court upheld the conviction and sentencing later.

No One Killed Jessica is a powerful reminder of the blatant misuse of the judiciary and police by India's political class and civil society's protests against that. That it was inspired by a newspaper headline is emblematic of the once-powerful anti-establishment nature of Indian media houses.

Mumbai is rocked by bomb blasts on a Tuesday

Neeraj Pandey used to work in television, and would write scripts for feature films in his spare time. On the last page of these scripts, he used to put his phone number down in the hope that whoever liked the script enough to reach the last page would call him. One night at 10.30 p.m., he got a call from a landline – from Naseeruddin Shah. Pandey had sent the script to Shah, but had lost all hope when his office informed him that Shah hadn't liked the script. Now he had arguably India's best actor on call, and Shah said he was willing to do his film.

That Pandey also got another thespian – Anupam Kher – to play Shah's foil and faced a lot of pressure to change his ageing cast for younger stars is part of film lore now. And it became film lore because the stark, hard-hitting script caught the pulse of the nation exactly right. *A Wednesday!* started from the blasts of July 2006, when seven bombs ripped through the suburban trains of Mumbai in a span of just 11 minutes. Two hundred and nine people never made it back home that Tuesday. With the premise of the common man getting killed every time a terrorist organization decides to target India, *A Wednesday!* is a thrilling 103-minute ride about the Mumbai Police Commissioner (Anupam Kher) racing against time to meet the demands of an unnamed adversary (Naseeruddin Shah) who wants four deadly terrorists released from custody.

Despite various challenges of finding a producer and then having a new producer come on board, *A Wednesday!* was ready in August 2007 – a year before it was finally released. The date was pushed because a suitable window to release the low-profile film couldn't be found, but when it did hit the screens, the film won over both the box office and the critics. More importantly, it started the trend of gritty terrorism thrillers, loosely inspired by real events, in Bollywood. *Mumbai Meri Jaan*, which released just before *A Wednesday!*, was on the human stories of the 2006 blasts. But – along with *Black Friday* that released in 2007 – *A Wednesday!* created the genre of slick, action-oriented, VFX-heavy chase-the-terrorist films, with a side of jingoism featured in films like *Kurbaan*, *New York*, *D-Day*, *Baby*, *Naam Shabana* and *Phantom*. What these films did was to take a real event of terror and spin a satisfying web of extracting revenge or drive home the futility of terror. This genre has now successfully spread its wings to the streaming platforms, and Neeraj Pandey's *Special Ops* continues this tradition.

Two-and-a-half months after *A Wednesday!* released, Mumbai faced another terrorist attack so shocking that it shook the security apparatus out of their slumber. Post that, a much more stringent security and monitoring apparatus was put in place, and India has managed to avert a similar attack on urban areas ever since. In an eerie coincidence, 26/11 was a Wednesday.

Om Shanti Om and *Saawariya* release on the same day

'Please support my film, a local production,' superstar Shah Rukh Khan humbly requested all the media persons and influencers he met in the run-up to the Diwali of 2007. A publicity blitz was underway to promote two films releasing on the same weekend – both with massive budgets and pre-release buzz. Shah Rukh's 'local' *Om Shanti Om* was up against *Saawariya*, the first Indian film to be fully financed by a Hollywood studio, Sony Pictures. And it was a battle royale on all fronts.

Sony Pictures pulled out all stops to promote its maiden Indian venture, releasing 750 trailer prints across India and 800 globally in the neo-digital world. This was the widest promotion for an Indian film. SRK – on the other hand – had got his six-pack abs and half of the industry in guest appearances, which were liberally promoted on all television channels.

Eid, Diwali and Christmas are the three major festival weekends, usually reserved for blockbusters with major stars. Producers and stars plan months in advance, and even arrive at a compromise to avoid clashes, because the first weekend is critical to a film's total box-office revenue. When films had a longer run, the first week clash was not a major factor and several blockbusters have released together in the past. So many sets of Sunny Deol's and Aamir Khan's earlier films – *Ghayal* and *Dil*, *Ghatak* and *Raja Hindustani*, *Gadar: Ek Prem Katha* and *Lagaan* – released together that it was considered something like a good luck charm. But by the time *Om Shanti Om* and *Saawariya* released, a clash was no longer desirable, but this particular contest couldn't be avoided due to ego conflicts at all levels. It, therefore, set up one of the most vaunted face-offs in Bollywood. It is not a spoiler to say that *Om Shanti Om* was a clear winner, and *Saawariya* – called 'an arthouse film made at the price of a blockbuster' – lost out to the pure Bollywood masala of songs, dances and rebirths. But *Om Shanti Om* lost on one front. Farah Khan claimed that the film would have been the first ever 100 crore–grosser at the domestic box-office if *Saawariya* hadn't taken away some of its business.

But that weekend's box-office wasn't the point. The point was the launch of three new stars – Ranbir Kapoor and Sonam Kapoor, from two of Bollywood's legendary industry families, and outsider Deepika Padukone, from a red-hot modelling career. In the subsequent two decades, all the three stars went on to rule the box-office, gossip columns and the mind space of Indian fans. At the time of their launch, the film press was abuzz with how Ranbir had worked as an assistant director in Sanjay Leela Bhansali's *Black* before being offered the lead in *Saawariya,* and how his role had shades of his famous grandfather. How Sonam Kapoor was selected over Alia Bhatt and Deepika Padukone. Deepika herself came recommended by fashion designer Wendell Rodricks during a Lakmé Fashion Week show, because Farah Khan was looking to launch a new actress opposite SRK. In the end, the battle was really between who would rule the next generation of Bollywood. Or, to paraphrase the tagline of *Om Shanti Om,* 'For some dreams, one generation is not enough'.

Wanted releases on Eid weekend

Salman Khan's life and career was in absolute disarray in the early-to-mid 2000s. After a hunting misadventure in 1998, he was involved in a driving accident in 2002 – where his car crushed four pavement dwellers, killing one of them. In 2005, a purported recording of his phone call with Aishwarya Rai surfaced, which indicated that he was involved with the Mumbai underworld. He had had an acrimonious breakup with Rai a few years back. His professional life wasn't much better either. All his films – barring one, *Partner* – between 2006 and 2008 had flopped.

Wanted, his first release of 2009, kept getting pushed back – first due to a multiplex strike (between April and June that year) and then to avoid clashes with other big releases. It was finally decided to release the film on the Eid-ul-Fitr weekend in September. Directed by Prabhu Deva, it was a remake of Telugu blockbuster *Pokiri*, which had also been made in Tamil. Probably because Salman's career was down in the dumps, he promoted the film extensively and even supported producer Boney Kapoor in a legal dispute to ensure the film's release.

Wanted took off like a rocket and ended up becoming the fourth-highest grosser of the year. Market reports indicated that the film went 'House Full' at single-screen theatres for the first time in ages, and some Mumbai theatres had to dig out their 'House Full' boards from storage rooms! Along with the business, it was the first step in building the cult of Salman Khan and the creation of his fanbase, who lap up everything their Bhai churns out. Multitudes of his young fans thronged single-screen theatres all over the country, making the film a huge hit despite poor critical reviews. After *Wanted*, this became both a template and timetable. Salman Khan and *Wanted* created the market for masala entertainers – studded with enough songs, action scenes, comedy tracks and melodrama to last you the coming week. *Wanted* was the first Salman Khan film planned for an Eid release and – after its massive success – every Eid since then has had a Bhai blockbuster.

Dabangg (2010), *Bodyguard* (2011), *Ek Tha Tiger* (2012), *Kick* (2014), *Bajrangi Bhaijaan* (2015) and *Sultan* (2016) were all Eid releases that were either the highest or second-highest grossing films of the year. Some are still among the highest-grossing Hindi films of all times. The last few years – *Tubelight* (2017), *Race 3* (2018), *Bharat* (2019) – have been somewhat disappointing, but only by Salman Khan's exalted standards. These films were all among the top 10 grossers of the years.

Salman Khan has made the Eid weekend his own – resurrecting both his career and image, while adding a 'big weekend' to the release calendar of Bollywood blockbusters. Even during a pandemic, *Radhe: Your Most Wanted Bhai* (a sequel of *Wanted*) released on a streaming platform on Eid, albeit to terrible reviews and unknown box-office numbers. And *Kabhi Eid Kabhi Diwali* is waiting for the next Eid. For diehard Salman Khan fans, the #BhaiRoxx hashtag isn't over yet.

Maharashtra Chief Minister watches *My Name is Khan*

A chief minister and home minister of a state watching the first day–first show of a film is a rare event, even in movie-crazy India. But Ashok Chavan and R.R. Patil of Maharashtra did exactly that when they drove down to Mumbai's Inox Fame Adlabs on a Friday to catch a show of Shah Rukh Khan–starrer *My Name is Khan*. On the same day, Shah Rukh Khan's wife, Gauri, watched the film at Fun Republic multiplex – again quite unprecedented for a celebrity to make it to a regular show. What they were all doing was to express confidence in the state's security apparatus after the Shiv Sena and Maharashtra Navnirman Sena (MNS) threatened to boycott and block the film's release.

It all started with the auction of players for the year's Indian Premier League (IPL). After several incidents of Pakistan-sponsored terrorism on Indian soil, there was pressure on IPL to not allow Pakistani players to play. While nothing was officially communicated, none of the teams bid for Pakistani players during the auction. After this, co-owner of Kolkata Knight Riders, Shah Rukh Khan, gave a statement that dropping Pakistani players from IPL was humiliating and that players should not be penalized for their state's actions. Almost immediately, the right-wing parties – most notably, the Shiv Sena – rose against Shah Rukh and demanded an apology. Which Shah Rukh refused to give. The demand for apology soon morphed into a threat to boycott his upcoming film, *My Name is Khan*, due about three weeks later.

To register their anger, Shiv Sena and its cousin party, MNS, threatened to disrupt the screening of the film. Multiplexes – fearing violent action from the parties' workers – unofficially postponed the advance booking of tickets. The Congress government of Maharashtra decided to show their administrative might and assured tight security at all multiplexes in the state. Calls for an apology from Shah Rukh grew more strident, while the government threatened to withdraw Shiv Sena leader Uddhav Thackeray's security for his unlawful behaviour. Mainstream and social media joined in, and the hashtag #MyNameIs started trending in solidarity with the film. The end result was an uneasy truce between Shah Rukh and Shiv Sena. The film released after some initial chaos. The chief minister watched the film. And the Sena workers were praised by their grand leader, Bal Thackeray, for their energetic opposition.

My Name is Khan was a typical case of intimidation of the film industry by political parties, where the former usually capitulated because of a potential business loss. It was atypical not only because the state government stepped in and offered protection to the film in question, but also because the star refused to apologize or alter his statement. This kind of intimidation continues across the political spectrum even today, usually without any support from the administration. And we wonder why Bollywood largely remains 'apolitical' and refuses to raise its voice against bad politics.

Sujoy Ghosh's short film *Ahalya* releases on YouTube

Sage Gautam had a very beautiful wife, Ahalya. The king of gods, Indra, took on the image of her husband and seduced her. When Gautam got to know of this, he cursed both Indra and Ahalya. The beautiful Ahalya was turned into a stone, who regained her human form only when Lord Rama's feet touched the stone. This mythological story from the Ramayana received a modern-day retelling with a twist, primarily because director Sujoy Ghosh wanted to work with legendary Bengali actor, Soumitra Chatterjee. The result was an enigmatic short film – which also had shades of a Satyajit Ray story – that simply made the genre explode when it released.

Ahalya, currently clocking 17.5 million views on YouTube, was the tipping point for short films in Hindi. Whiskey brand Royal Stag sponsors a series called *Large Short Films,* featuring big names as directors and actors. Even before *Ahalya,* the series had Anurag Kashyap and Sudhir Mishra making short films. Kashyap's film on the ghastly impact of roadside sexual harassment also drew a lot of eyeballs, but Ghosh's film is probably more representative of the strengths of the genre. It shows how a digital short film can reach a national audience, despite being in a regional language (Bengali) and based on unfamiliar sources.

Large Short Films – as a channel – started in 2012 and a high-profile anthology of four short films by major directors, *Bombay Talkies,* released in theatres in 2013. As did Anurag Kashyap's first short film, *That Day After Everyday.* But the frequency and promotion both picked up after *Ahalya.* The next big boost was *Chutney,* produced and co-written by actress Tisca Chopra, and directed by Jyoti Kapur Das. The 'creepy and understated' *Chutney* went totally viral in November 2016 and reached a massive 128 million views on YouTube. Neeraj Ghaywan, director of the acclaimed *Masaan,* had cut his film-making teeth before his feature debut. He came back to the medium right

afterwards with *Juice*, a scathing commentary on casual patriarchy.

You know something has created an impact in Bollywood when Filmfare institutes an award for it. Filmfare duly started awards specifically for short films, from 2016 onwards. Manoj Bajpayee won the Best Actor for *Taandav*, in which he played a dancing cop (which, in turn, was based on a viral video). Tisca Chopra was Best Actress for *Chutney*. In subsequent years, the acting awards have gone to both stars (Jackie Shroff, Shefali Shah) as well as newcomers (Hussain Dalal, Kirti Kulhari). With streaming platforms and online film clubs, revenue options have multiplied and with this, so has the market for short films. Like the mythological Ahalya, the genre has come back to life.

Baahubali 2: The Conclusion releases nationally

'Why did Katappa kill Baahubali? *Katappa ne Baahubali ko kyun maara?*' Over nearly two years, this question spread across India to become the subject of fan theories, frenzied internet discussion, social media posts, jokes, gags, memes and eventually the publicity campaign of *Baahubali 2: The Conclusion* – the film with the highest box-office revenue in domestic markets.

The makers of *Baahubali: The Beginning* decided to leverage the pan-India appeal of their offering by having Karan Johar's Dharma Productions as the distributor for the Hindi-dubbed version. Karan Johar, a one-man marketing machine, upped the profile of director S.S. Rajamouli to a miracle maker, which was duly proved by the humongous success of the two films.

Baahubali 2 was an avalanche of new records – highest number of trailer views, widest release for an Indian film, highest first day/weekend/fortnight collections – on the back of that rare feat: A sequel meeting expectations of the first part; not to mention the even rarer feat of being a truly crossover film in India. Remakes of South Indian films often do well in the North, but this was a dubbed version – with not-so-well-known Telugu stars – winning audiences all over. A key reason was that various plot elements were similar to the familiar tales of the Ramayana and Mahabharata. A dutiful scion being exiled, a prince abandoned at birth, a princess falling in love with an incognito prince, an army of renegades fighting against tyrannical powers – these are stories all Indians are familiar with. Reviewers saw similarities with the visual style of *Baahubali* and childhood favourites like *Amar Chitra Katha* and *Chandamama,* which made the films doubly identifiable.

The *Baahubali* franchise also started that rare phenomenon of creating an industry around its characters, events and locations. A tour of the *Baahubali* film sets is a thing at Hyderabad's Ramoji Film City. An official online merchandise store is live. An online multiplayer game was launched. An animated series – featuring the growing up years of Amarendra Baahubali and Bhallaladeva – is also available. And what is probably the biggest extension, a trilogy of prequel stories is being produced as Netflix originals with a global release. *Baahubali: Before the Beginning* is based on *The Rise of Sivagami*, the childhood story of the queen.

Baahubali was South Indian cinema conquering North Indian audiences. It was Indian mythology-fantasy wowing Western audiences. It was great marketing backing phenomenal storytelling and technology. It was the biggest gamble Indian cinema took (with a budget of ₹430 crores) and became a towering triumph. Also, it was the story of why someone lovingly raised a boy only to kill him as an adult!

Sacred Games drops on Netflix

Ashwathama. Halahal. Atapi Vatapi. Brahmahatya. Sarama. Pretakalpa. Rudra. Yayati.

When *Sacred Games* was launched as the first Netflix original from India – after a massive marketing campaign – the country's internet was awash with deep analyses about these eight names from Hindu mythology. They were the titles of the eight episodes of season 1 and the discussions were representative of the craze that the series generated in India.

Netflix predicts their next 100 million users will come from India, and they began their foray into Indian content creation with a voluminous 2006 novel. Vikramaditya Motwane (then running Phantom Films) was approached to film the 900-page novel as a series, and he got the writers on board to begin the scripting process. Anurag Kashyap, who had read and loved the novel when it first came out, came on board as a co-director – shooting the parts featuring Ganesh Gaitonde (Nawazuddin Siddiqui), while Motwane shot the parts with Sartaj Singh (Saif Ali Khan).

Kashyap and Motwane have a small but loyal fan base, who are active online and generate a lot of buzz for the releases. However, the frenzied speculation over *Sacred Games* was something else altogether. For starters, the first season was nearly seven hours long and had long character arcs, slow-burning mysteries and intricate production design for fans to salivate on. Apart from the cinematic value, there was significant titillation as well, with profanity, sex and nudity burning up the screen. A saga that mixed crime, politics, religion, business, glamour and espionage, *Sacred Games* stepped on a lot of political toes. It attacked many a holy cow, including a mildly abusive comment ('*fattu*') for former Prime Minister Rajiv Gandhi, which was subtitled as 'pussy'. It also showed how communal passions were fanned in India of the 1990s – something never seen before in a mainstream Bollywood production.

Sacred Games was a great start for Netflix in India. Both the form and content struck a chord, and accelerated both the

viewing of and production for steaming platforms in India. For film-makers, streaming platforms offered an international market of massive scale. *Sacred Games* was shown in 191 countries, easily the biggest release for an Indian production, and two-thirds of its viewers were from outside the country, a triumph for Indian content on global streaming platforms.

Strictly speaking, Hotstar was India's first streaming platform and is still the leader in terms of users. However, the competition started heating up ever since Netflix and Amazon Prime Video launched in 2016, followed by dozens of others. Apart from the viewing habits of users, what they changed is also the way Bollywood works. All major production houses are now actively creating content that reach a much larger audience and allow much more creative freedom. After years of submitting to the whims and fancies of a conservative 'censor board', Indian film-makers are now getting used to calling political leaders names and getting away with it.[12] F***, yeah!

---

12. Not fully, because the government has now woken up, and is looking to create a strict self-regulation framework and censorship rules for OTT platforms in India.

Tanushree Dutta accuses Nana Patekar of sexual harassment

If we took sexual harassment allegations seriously, India's #MeToo movement would have started in March 2008, when former Miss India Tanushree Dutta accused Nana Patekar of sexually harassing on the sets of *Horn 'Ok' Pleassss.* She said that Patekar grabbed her arms, pushed her around and got new dance steps introduced that required her to be physically more intimate with him. When she refused and left the shoot, a mob – allegedly on Patekar's instigation – vandalized her car. She filed a complaint in 2008 and repeated the allegation in 2013, but was ignored. It was only in the context of the global #MeToo movement in 2018 that she was finally heard and an FIR was filed. And Bollywood exploded in a mushroom cloud of harassment allegations – some of them years old.

Hrithik Roshan–starrer *Super 30*. Akshay Kumar–starrer *Housefull 4*. Aamir Khan–starrer *Mogul*. Three of Bollywood's biggest productions got derailed because of accusations against their directors. Vikas Bahl was accused of harassing a woman crew member while shooting *Queen* – ironically a film on women's empowerment. Sajid Khan was accused of repeatedly harassing an assistant director. Subhash Kapoor was accused by an actress who had even filed an FIR against him in 2014, but he was granted bail and has made three films since then. In a stunning revelation, a writer–producer accused Alok Nath – known for his 'father' roles – of raping her in the mid-1990s. Beyond these, there were a flurry of allegations – against the likes of Vivek Agnihotri, Kailash Kher, Anu Malik – and, for a while, it seemed that very few people in Bollywood would have their reputations intact. And unlike regular harassment complaints, most survivors didn't keep their identities a secret and openly came out – even at the risk of retaliation. The #MeToo movement spread to regional film industries as well as the peripheries of the film industry. In one of the most high-profile cases, Tamil singer Chinmayi Sripada accused lyricist Vairamuthu of harassment, while comedy collective All India

Bakchod folded after their mishandling of a complaint came to light.

It is ironical that biggest impact of #MeToo was seen not on the perpetrators, but on the abettors, or more accurately, the bystanders who didn't do enough. Like AIB, production house Phantom Films (comprising Anurag Kashyap, Vikramaditya Motwane and Madhu Mantena, apart from Vikas Bahl) shut shop after they apologized for not taking the complaint against Bahl seriously enough. But the accused themselves had no concrete action taken against them – sometimes for lack of evidence and sometimes due to the absence of a formal complaint itself. Observers felt that the #MeToo movement sensitized the industry and sexual harassment guidelines are now being implemented, more so due to multi-national corporates running production companies in Bollywood. But in a depressingly symbolic move, the Mumbai Police closed the case against Nana Patekar after informing the courts that there was no evidence to prosecute him.

Gulabo Sitabo releases on Amazon Prime Video

A form of puppet theatre in Uttar Pradesh pits two women against each other. Sometimes they are two sisters-in-law bickering in the same household, sometimes they are the wife and mistress of the same man vying for his attention. Created by Ram Niranjan Lal Srivastava of Pratapgarh in Uttar Pradesh, the puppets fought viciously while passing on some social message to the audience. These puppets were called Gulabo and Sitabo.

After nearly two months of a Covid-19–induced lockdown in India – when cinema theatres were shut and new releases were pushed indefinitely – Amazon Prime Video announced a coup that is likely to change how cinema is exhibited and viewed in India. Shoojit Sircar's *Gulabo Sitabo* was acquired for exhibition on the streaming platform and it became the first film meant for a theatrical release that went direct-to-streaming. And started a battle – reminiscent of the eponymous puppets.

For starters, multiplex chains were up in arms against this attack on their business. Inox Movies expressed 'extreme displeasure and disappointment', and threatened to take 'retributive measures against such fair-weather friends'. PVR Cinemas was less vitriolic and reminded everyone that a theatrical release was the 'best way for audiences to experience the labour and creative genius of our film-makers'. The film-makers – on the other hand – expressed their inability to hold on for an indefinite period of time without a return on their investments.

Gulabo Sitabo wasn't the only film to be acquired by streaming services. Between Amazon Prime and Netflix, a slew of announcements were made about films with major stars that were now going to be aired on the streaming services. Vidya Balan–starrer *Shakuntala Devi*, Janhvi Kapoor–starrer *Gunjan Saxena: The Kargil Girl* and Akshay Kumar–starrer *Laxmi Bomb* among others were announced almost at the same time, and many more are in the pipeline. But entertainers on a grand scale – like Rohit Shetty's *Sooryavanshi* and Kabir Khan's *83* – held back, waiting for theatres to reopen. Which leads to an interesting demarcation between those films that could bypass a theatrical release and the films that won't.

Gulabo Sitabo released at midnight, and changed the concept of the 'first-day-first-show' timing. It also got some rapturous reviews from major critics, while some viewers felt the film was too slow. This also led to the speculation about how well the film would have done with a theatrical release and whether this was the right strategy for them. Just like Amitabh Bachchan and Ayushmann Khurrana's bickering in *Gulabo Sitabo,* the tug-of-war between theatres and streaming services is likely to be long drawn. And just the same way cinema watching went from 35 mm to 70 mm to video parlour to television, the mobile phone is likely to be the next premiere venue. Grab your popcorn buckets!

Bibliography

Akhtar, Javed and Nasreen Munni Kabir. *Talking Films: Conversations on Hindi Cinema with Javed Akhtar*. New Delhi: Oxford University Press, 2014.

Bashir, Saba Mahmood. *Gulzar's Aandhi: Insights into the Film*. Noida: Harper Collins Publishers India, 2019.

Bhatia, Uday. Bullets Over Bombay: Satya and the Hindi Film Gangster. Noida: Harper Collins Publishers India, 2021.

Chintamani, Gautam. *Qayamat Se Qayamat Tak: The Film That Revived Hindi Cinema*. Noida: Harper Collins Publishers India, 2016.

Chopra, Vidhu Vinod and Abhijat Joshi. *Unscripted: Conversations on Life and Cinema*. Gurgaon: Penguin Random House, 2021.

Desai, Kishwar. *The Life and Times of Devika Rani: The Longest Kiss*. Chennai: Westland Publications, 2020.

De Shobha. *Selective Memory: Stories from My Life*. Gurgaon: Penguin, 2015.

Garga, Bhagwan Das. *So Many Cinemas: The Motion Picture in India*. Mumbai: Eminence Designs, 1996.

Gooptu, Sharmistha, Avijit Ghosh and Srijana Mitra Das. *Flashback: 175 Years of Entertainment Entertainment Entertainment*. New Delhi: Bennet, Coleman & Co. Ltd, 2013.

Johar, Karan and Poonam Saxena. *An Unsuitable Boy*. Gurgaon: Penguin Random House, 2018.

Majumdar, Neepa. *Wanted Cultured Ladies Only!: Female Stardom and Cinema in India, 1930s-1950s*. University of Illinois Press, 2010.

Menon, Suresh. *Pataudi: Nawab of Cricket*. Noida: Harper Collins Publishers India, 2013.

Mukerjea, Peter. *Star Struck: Confessions of a TV Executive*. Chennai: Westland Business, 2021.

Mukherjee, Debashree. *Bombay Hustle: Making Movies in a Colonial City*. New York: Columbia University Press, 2020.

Mukherjee, Ram Kamal. *Hema Malini: Beyond the Dream Girl: An Authorized Biography*. Noida: Harper Collins Publishers India, 2017.

Pinto, Jerry. *Helen: The Life and Times of an H-Bomb*. New Delhi: Penguin , 2006.

Pinto, Jerry. *The Greatest Show on Earth: Writings on Bollywood*. New Delhi: Penguin Books, 2011.

Rajagopalan, Sudha. *Leave Disco Dancer Alone!: Indian Cinema and Soviet Movie-Going after Stalin*. New Delhi: Yoda Press, 2008.

Reuben, Bunny. *Follywood Flashback: A Collection of Movie Memories*. New Delhi: Harper Collins Publications India, 1993.

Saran, Sathya. *Ten Years with Guru Dutt: Abrar Alvi's Journey*. Gurgaon: Penguin Random House, 2020.

Singh, Tavleen. *Durbar*. Gurgaon: Hachette India, 2013.

Usman, Yasser. *Sanjay Dutt: The Crazy Untold Story of Bollywood's Bad Boy*. New Delhi: Juggernaut, 2018.

Vatave, Bapu. *Dadasaheb Phalke, the Father of Indian Cinema*. New Delhi: National Book Trust, 2004.

Acknowledgements

Akhil Jain, Bhaskar Jyoti Dey and Neeraj Ghaywan for their help with sourcing the images.

Thomas Abraham, Poulomi Chatterjee, Swarnima Narayan and Ansila Thomas of Hachette India, for indulging me at every turn and turning my ramblings into a dream series.

Echo Chamber, Sobuj Sangho, Kwiz Group, for fuelling many trivial pursuits.

Rita Chaudhuri, Shivaramakrishnan K and Nilendu Misra, for always being ready to talk movies.

Trishna, Dyujoy and Drishti Chaudhuri, for always being there.